Capital Cities of Arab Islam

*T*he contribution of the McKnight Foundation to the general program of the University of Minnesota Press, of which the publication of this book is a part, is gratefully acknowledged

Capital Cities
of
Arab Islam

By
Philip K. Hitti

UNIVERSITY OF MINNESOTA PRESS
Minneapolis

Library of Congress Catalog Card Number: 72-92335

ISBN 0-8166-0663-3

The maps on pages 5 and 113 are reprinted from *History of the Arabs*, © 1937, by permission of Macmillan, London, and St. Martin's Press, New York. The maps on pages 20–21, 50–51, 77, 129, and 137 are reprinted from *Makers of Arab History*, © 1968 by Philip K. Hitti, by permission of Macmillan, London; St. Martin's Press, New York; and Mr. Joseph Ascherl. The poems on pages 144 and 158 are reprinted from *A Literary History of the Arabs* by Reynold A. Nicholson, © 1966, by permission of Cambridge University Press.

Preface

*T*his is an attempt to view the highlights of Arab history through the windows of the cities where those events were enacted. The study therefore is more historical than geographical, and is addressed to the student and cultured layman rather than to the specialist. In its compilation the author drew upon some of the research material he had prepared for his earlier works, particularly his *History of the Arabs* and *History of Syria Including Lebanon and Palestine*. The six cities treated were more than capitals; they left their indelible imprint not only on the subsequent history of the Arabs and Moslems but on the development of civilization at large. The study hopes to arouse the interest of the reader, but does not claim to satisfy it.

Several cities studied in this book were revisited by the author while enjoying with his wife the hospitality of his sister and brother-in-law Nabihah and Najib Jabbur in their Shimlan summer home, Lebanon, in the 1960s.

P. K. H.

Princeton, N.J.

v

Pilgrim at the Kaabah, Mecca

Table
of
Contents

Capital Cities of Arab Islam

1
Mecca:
The Religious Capital

Our Lord, I have made some of my seed dwell in a
valley with no sown land by Thy Holy House [the
Kaabah] so that, O Lord, they may perform
prayers. Make then some hearts of men turn to
them and make provision of fruit for them, haply
they may be thankful.

Abraham in the Koran

It all began with a well. The well lay in an
uncultivated valley and the valley in a barren land. Zamzam was the
well's name, Hijaz the land's name. The Zamzam water was briny but
in the scorched throat of a Bedouin, no sweet water could have tasted
sweeter.

To the tribe which in remote antiquity settled around the Zamzam,
the water which first supplied a vital need became in due course endowed with some mysterious, magical power. So it did in the experience of earlier Semitic and non-Semitic tribes. In many primitive
cultures, East and West, water figured in magico-religious cults. It
occupied a prominent place in the Hebrew ceremonial system. Priests
were washed at their consecration (Ex. 29:4); they washed their hands
and feet before offering sacrifices (Ex. 30:18–21) and on certain occasions special ablutions were required (Lev. 16:4, 24). Washing was used
for removing ceremonial defilement (Lev. 11:32; 15:5 seq.), but in connection with leprosy and other forms of uncleanliness running water
was required (Lev. 14:5–6, 50–52). Christians continued the tradition

3

by the use of water for purification from sin, as in baptism, and Moslems by its employment for cleanliness from defilement, as in ablution, a prerequisite of legal prayer. Allah enhanced the importance of this liquid by declaring in the Koran (21:31): "And of water have We made everything living."

A member of that Arabian tribe which settled near the Zamzam hit in the neighborhood upon a stone conspicuous by its difference. It was black. Other stones nearby were not. Strangeness inspired awe. Awe led to veneration. Veneration ended in endowing the object with something unique, some supernatural power. At first the black stone was sheltered perhaps in a tent. In course of time a house was built for the sacred object. The structure was cube-like in form, whence its Arabic name Ka'bah (Kaabah). Though enlarged and modified in the course of centuries the structure maintained its form and its name. There was nothing unique in this Arabian tribal experience. Other primitive men in Europe and Asia were inclined to treat similar findings in a similar manner and ultimately to incorporate them into their magico-religious cults. They were right in the sense that such stones, being meteoritic, descended from heaven.

When Jacob had his nocturnal encounter with Jehovah he set up the stone on which he had laid his head for a pillar, poured oil on it, and called it Beth-El (house of God, Gen. 28:18–19; the Kaabah was also so called). In several other cases stones were consecrated as memorials to the Hebrew deity and as altars (1 Sam. 7:12; cf. Is. 19:19; Judg. 6:20; 13:19). Not only were certain stones and rocks considered sacred but they were worshiped as idols. At times so widespread was the practice that Jehovah found it necessary to admonish his people vehemently against it: "Ye shall make you no idols nor graven image, neither rear you up a standing image, neither shall ye set up any image of stone in your land, to bow down unto it" (Lev. 26:1; cf. Deut. 29:17; 2 Kings 19:18; Is. 57:6).

I

The first recorded mention of Mecca takes the form of Macoraba and occurs in the geography of the Greco-Egyptian scientist Ptolemy, written in Alexandria about the mid-second Christian century. The form is South Arabic (Sabaean) and indicates pre-Christian beginnings when

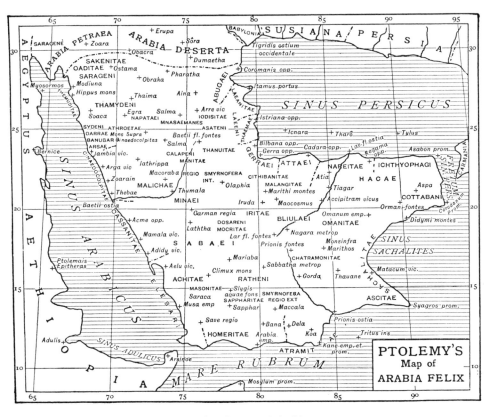

Ptolemy's map of Arabia

Arabians from Yaman controlled the trade routes. The Yamanis were the Phoenicians of the Arabian Sea. Their country was one of the few areas in the Peninsula favored with enough rainfall to warrant cultivation. It and its neighbor Hadramawt produced spices, incense, and other tropical products in great demand in lands to the north. In days before refrigeration condiments were used not only for flavoring, seasoning, and giving zest to food but for preserving it. Macoraba was one of the stations on the spice-incense route. A town grew around the sanctuary. The sanctuary became a center of a cult and an object of pilgrimage. The area around the sanctuary became a forbidden and inviolable asylum providing refuge and immunity. The name Macoraba meant "house of the Lord." Mecca (Makkah) then had a long history as a sanctuary and a trade center before Islam.

Surprisingly, the Koran makes no mention by that name of the city that became the chief center of its faith. The form it gives the name is

5

Bakkah (the *m* and *b* in South Arabic are interchangeable), and that is mentioned only once in surah (chapter) 3:90: "Verily the first house established for the people was that at Bakkah, a house blessed and a guidance to all the world." The following verse says: "Therein are clear evidences — the station of Abraham and the security for him who enters it," a clear reference to the Kaabah. This rendered the area around the sanctuary *haram* (forbidden, sacred), corresponding to the Levitical city of refuge in the Old Testament. Another koranic reference (6:92; 42:5) to Mecca makes it Umm al-Qura (mother of all settlements).

The Koran further ascribes the building of the Kaabah to Abraham (Ibrahim) in collaboration with his son Ishmael (Isma'il, 2:118–119). It makes the religion of Abraham the precursor of the religion of Muhammad and the Kaabah its palladium. More poetical traditionists ascribe the first building to the angels and the second to Adam. As for Zamzam, now one hundred and forty feet deep and crowned with an elegant dome, it was dug by Angel Gabriel to save the lives of Hagar (Hajar) and her son Ishmael (cf. Gen. 21:19) as they were lost in the waterless desert. The Black Stone, Gabriel's gift to Abraham, is now lodged in the east corner of the Kaabah five feet above the ground. It is twelve inches in diameter and its surface is worn smooth by kissing.

In the Arabian Peninsula the southern part, favored with rain and rich in spices, aromatic herbs, and frankincense, was the first to step on the threshold of history. Its people differed from North Arabians in language and religion. For centuries before Christ they had flourished under governments of the monarchic type, and monopolized trade in their own products as well as those of Abyssinia, India, and the Far East. Exotic products found their way by land and sea into the Yaman and Hadramawt markets. For a time the shrewd Arabian merchants were able to keep the foreign sources secret, leaving the impression that all were native.

The Roman conquest of Arabia's northern neighbors in the first century B.C. gave South Arabian trade a fresh impetus. It expanded its market to the entire Mediterranean basin. The new customers became the greatest consumers of Arabian offerings. The Romans, like the Near Easterners before them, employed condiments to mask disagreeable odors and to camouflage the taste of foods partially decomposed.

Once a luxury, the "spices of Araby" became a necessity when people grew accustomed to them.

Of all this Mecca was a beneficiary. Its location at the crossing of the Yaman-Syria and the Yaman-Iraq routes gave it a special advantage. To the Yaman depots, Hadramawt offered frankincense in demand for embalming the dead in Egypt and for perfuming temples and Christian churches. Southeastern Arabia furnished perfume and aromatic gums, while the Persian Gulf furnished its pearls. China supplied silk and India fabrics, condiments, and swords. Abyssinia served as a source for slaves, gold, ivory, and other luxury products. In the Peninsula the one-humped, long-suffering, undemanding camel was, of course, the main means of transportation. It could carry five hundred pounds, cover twenty-five miles a day, and survive for days on a minimal supply of food and water.

The camel was an indispensable member of the Arabian caravan. As the caravan moved northward it picked up animal skins from Bedouin Hijaz and raisins from Ta'if, Mecca's summer resort. The ships of the desert connected with the ships of the sea at the ports of Palestine and Lebanon, whence other ports in the Mediterranean basin were reached. On the way back the caravan carried glass and metalware, cotton goods, olive oil, wine, and dried fruits. To the Meccans, whose barren city was hemmed in by a double range of steep and uncultivable hills, the caravan business was indeed a godsend. An early snapshot of an Arabian caravan has been preserved in Genesis 37:25, relating to Joseph's sale of his brethren to Ishmaelites with "camels bearing spicery and balm and myrrh." Starting as service station men, Meccans developed into retailers, dealers, and by the time of Muhammad into financiers and caravaneers. They additionally served as middlemen exchanging commodities with local Bedouins.

Caravan trade was a more complicated business than appears on the surface. Besides finances, training, and experience, it involved knowledge of geography and of facilities for supplying water and relaying mounts. Guides and guards were necessary, so were alliances — at least forms of understanding with tribes whose territories lay en route. Passage often entailed payment of tolls, taxes, or bribes. Escorts were reinforced on passing through a hostile territory. A caravan might consist of hundreds of camels and scores of merchants. Its departure and its return must have provided special occasions for the gathering of curious spectators, Bedouin and urbanite. The Koran (106:2) refers to two Meccan caravans, one in summer and one in winter. Merchants counted on up to a hundred per cent profit to meet expenses and ensure the proper yield on their investment.

II

Mecca entered upon its first era of peace and prosperity when the Quraysh tribe — later ennobled by the birth of the Prophet Muhammad in it — occupied it around the mid–fifth century of the Christian era. Tradition credits the feat to a semilegendary ancestor named Qusayy. Qusayy was said to have united the scattered clans — fictitious or genuine — of the Quraysh under his chieftainship, installed them by a coup de main in the center of Mecca, and gained possession of its sanctuary. He, in the words of an Italian orientalist, was for Mecca what Romulus was for Rome. Not only did he expand the Kaabah but he organized its rite and developed certain functions related to it and to its city. Chief among these were the guardianship and holding the keys of the Kaabah (*hijabah*), providing drinking water, particularly during the pilgrimage, with special reference to the Zamzam (*siqayah*), and supplying those of the pilgrims who needed it with food (*rifadah*). The pilgrim in Islam was styled Allah's guest (*dayf Allah*), and if he lingered for some time he was called Allah's neighbor (*mujawir*). For him the Kaabah custodians felt special responsibility.

To this early hero of the Quraysh is also ascribed the building of a public hall (*dar al-nadwah*) by the Kaabah in which members of the Quraysh above forty years of age would meet to discuss municipal or religious problems of common concern. In this council chamber tribal marriages were arranged and the flag (*liwa'*) was bestowed by the chief on the military leader. The council was probably more deliberative than executive. Final decisions and executions were in the chieftain's hands and were passed after him to his descendants. There was enough sanctity in the Kaabah to impart sanctity not only on the surrounding area but also on its custodians.

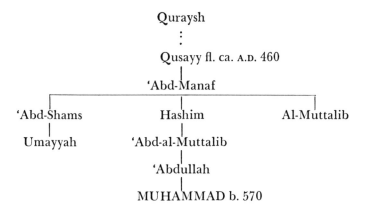

Quraysh
⋮
Qusayy fl. ca. A.D. 460
|
'Abd-Manaf
|
'Abd-Shams   Hashim   Al-Muttalib
| |
Umayyah   'Abd-al-Muttalib
|
'Abdullah
|
MUHAMMAD b. 570

On the eve of Muhammad's birth Mecca must have evolved into a merchant republic, a precursor of Venice, Pisa, and Genoa. The Quraysh were its merchant princes. Yaman's conquest by Abyssinia, approximately half a century before Muhammad's birth, contributed to that end. It opened before Meccans fresh avenues for exercising their commercial and financial talents. They then began to organize and finance their own caravans and establish their own trading stations from Najran in northern Yaman to the land of the Nabataeans in southern Palestine. Originally of South Arabian stock, the Abyssinians had by this time been Christianized. The Abyssianian governor Abraha (Abraham) built a cathedral in the Yamani capital San'a', represented by Arab authors as an incomparable piece of architecture, intended as a rival to the Kaabah. These historians go on to say that the Abyssinian attack on Mecca in 570 had as its aim the destruction of that sanctuary. The rivalry was probably more economic than religious. What the Abyssinians desired to destroy was probably the Meccans' position as middlemen in the south-to-north international trade. The invaders used an elephant, which was as much of a horrifying innovation to the enemy as the use of the tank in the First World War or the nuclear weapon in the Second. The elephant (Ar. *fil*) gave its name to a short surah in the Koran:

> Hast thou not seen how thy Lord did with the owners
>   of the elephant?
> Did He not make their scheme go astray?
> He loosed upon them birds in flocks,

9

Which pelted them with stones of baked clay,
Which left them like devoured green blades.

105:1–5

The episode is reminiscent of the Assyrian attack on Jerusalem in 701 B.C., when according to the Hebrew version the Lord sent His angel to smite the enemy and save the city (2 Chron. 32:21–22). It was probably smallpox that saved the Kaabah; the bubonic plague saved the Temple.

III

The birth of Muhammad (570) in Mecca was the first fact that distinguished it above its contemporaries and made of it a city of destiny. The "descent" of the first surahs of revelation in it forty years later was the second most pregnant fact in its history. The descent raised Mecca to a unique position of greatness. The two facts combine to give the barren city of Hijaz a niche in the hall of immortals.

The precise circumstances under which the Arabian Prophet received his call are not clear. Koranic commentators generally agree that surah 96 was the first to descend:

Read in the name of thy Lord who created,
created man from a clot of blood.
Read, for thy Lord is the most bounteous
who teacheth by the pen,
Teacheth man what he did not know.

96:1–5

Muhammad's biographer ibn-Hisham, the leading classical historian al-Tabari, and others agree that the scene was a cave in a mount outside Mecca called Hira', which had provided the distraught, agitated candidate with a retreat for contemplation. It was there that he heard a voice, later identified as that of Gabriel. One may guess that for some time Muhammad must have been pondering the problem of reading sacred books, which Jews and Christians were able to do but he was not. Hence the first command: "Read." And as if the startled addressee asked how he could read when he had had no schooling, the command was repeated with some explanation. Hira' has since been styled the Mount of Light, and the night of revelation has been fixed

as one of the last ones of Ramadan, the ninth month of the lunar year
(2:181). The night is characterized in the Koran (97) as the Night of
Power.

Two further developments enhanced the prestige of Mecca and have
kept its name alive on the tongues and in the hearts of believers the
world over: prayer and pilgrimage. The Prophet chose it as the direction (*qiblah*, kiblah) to which Moslems should turn while reciting
their five daily prescribed prayers. "Turn your face toward the Holy
Mosque [in Mecca], and wherever ye are turn your faces in its direction" (2:139). This injunction was revealed to Muhammad shortly
after his arrival at Medina, before which Jerusalem had been used by
him as the kiblah. Thus, for a Moslem to render his prayer acceptable,
he should be oriented Mecca-ward.

Pilgrimage to Mecca is also prescribed in the Koran. It gives Mecca
a place among other centers of pilgrimage, such as Jerusalem, Rome,
and Benares, but its place remains unique. Pilgrimaging to it is considered an act of worship incumbent on every believer who can afford
it once in a lifetime. It occurs at a stated time and collectively. In no
other center is pilgrimage so ritualized and institutionalized as in the
Islamic center. Its mandatory character is revealed in the Koran:

> Fulfill the major and the minor pilgrimages unto Allah.
> But if ye are prevented,
>   then make such as may be feasible.
> And shave not your heads
>   till the offering reaches its destination.
> If any of you is sick or injured in the head,
>   then a compensation by fasting, almsgiving, or
>   other pious observation.
>   2:192

Even today the holy pilgrimage is considered a central aim in a pious
life, and its achievement a culminating point in religiosity. Many
Moslems who observe neither the daily prayer nor the fast of Ramadan
participate in this act of worship. Any hardships or privations endured are but a small price to pay. He who undertakes it can thereafter proudly affix the honorific title of *hajj* before his name. The increased facilities of communications have in recent years swelled the
number of annual pilgrims to a million.

The annual pilgrimage at a stated month, dhu-al-Hijjah (the twelfth month in the lunar calendar Moslems use), is the major one cited in the koranic quotation. The minor one (*'umrah*) may be undertaken individually at any time of the year. While the goal in both cases is Mecca, many visitors — collectively or individually — take advantage of the opportunity to visit its sister Medina. There, they pray briefly and not so ceremoniously at the Prophet's Mosque, the one Muhammad built. The minor pilgrimage is not a mandatory but a meritorious act of worship (2:153). In both major and minor pilgrimages, the visitor should be in a state of consecration (*ihram*). Ritual purity requires, besides an ablution involving the whole body, abstinence from sex relations and shedding blood. It also requires shaving or trimming the beard, cutting the nails, and perfuming the body. A white seamless garment is worn and only sandals are allowed. The head remains uncovered.

The annual visitations give Mecca the opportunity for self-renewal. As the season approaches, the city scrubs its face, dons its holiday attire, and spreads the red carpet to welcome its guests — the guests of Allah. For few days as Arabs, Persians and Turks, Pakistanis, Afghanis and Indians, Chinese, Malayans and Indonesians, Sudanese, Senegalese and other Africans flock to it; it presents a microcosm of the Islamic world.

Neither orientation in prayer nor visitation of sacred places originated in Islam. Daniel in his land of exile turned his face toward Jerusalem as he prayed (Dan. 6:10). The early Christian churches were oriented eastward. The entire institution of pilgrimage in Arabia was pre-Islamic in origin. Almost all the ceremonies connected with it were practiced by heathen Arabians. Only the prayers were introduced and the interpretation changed. The system was Islamized. Muhammad could not divorce himself entirely from his background no matter how hard he tried. Besides, there were his conservative fellow countrymen, whom he wanted to attract. In adopting the Kaabah and the pilgrimage he made his greatest concession to paganism and alienated his monotheism from its two sisters.

Tradition added its quota to the exaltation of the Prophet's birthplace and the scene of his revelation. Books and books have been authored through the ages on the excellences (*fada'il*) of Mecca. They leave no doubt that its people are endowed with special virtues; one day in it is worth an age elsewhere; prayer therein is more meritorious than anywhere else; and death in Mecca is preferable to death in any other city. That a city with oppressive climate, saline water, uncomfortably lodged in a barren valley, and with a population that dishonorably repudiated the son who gave it its claim to greatness should be entitled *al-Mukarramah* (the highly honored) is one of the ironies of history.

There was no reason why Mecca should take note of a boy born in it in 570 to an impoverished clan of the Quraysh, a boy bereaved of one parent before his birth and of the other before he was six. The lad was brought up by an uncle, abu-Talib, and there was nothing to indicate that he would grow to differ from any of his contemporaries. His marriage at the age of twenty-five to a wealthy widow of his tribe, Khadijah, gave him the first taste of economic sufficiency. Khadijah was in the caravan business and he was first her employee.

The Rubicon was not crossed till 610 when the forty-year-old caravaneer proclaimed himself a prophet of Allah. There was nothing startling in that. Polytheism by its nature is more tolerant of prophets and can accommodate more deities than monotheism. Besides, Allah was an honored god of the Kaabah. Muhammad's father bore his name, 'Abdullah (the slave of Allah). What was startling was the implications of the message as it began to unfold itself. The Allah (Ar. *al-Ilah*, the god) whom Muhammad preached was the only true god; all others were false. He was the creator, self-sustainer, omnipotent, omnipresent, omniscient. This Allah had chosen Muhammad to be His last and greatest prophet. He had thus addressed him:

> Say: He is God alone,
> God, the eternal,
> He begetteth not,
> Nor is He begotten,
> And none is comparable unto Him.
>
> 112

To him who obeys Allah's commands, as communicated to His messenger, attractive rewards are offered in Paradise; but to him who disobeys, nothing but fire in Hell is prepared. The day of judgment was imminent. Full submission (*islam*, whence the name of the new religion) was a prerequisite. The oneness of God thus became the corner-

13

stone of Islam; the teachings that there is no god whatever but Allah (*la ilaha illa-l-Lah*) and Muhammad is the messenger of Allah (*Muhammadun rasulu-l-Lah*) became and remained the motto of the new religion.

Clearly, in all this novel teaching, Judaeo-Christian ideas are reflected. Mecca had no Christian colony but had Christian slaves and visitors. South of Hijaz lay Najran, which had been Christian for centuries. Christianized Arabian tribes (Ghassan) flourished on the eastern border of Syria, and others on the southern border of Iraq. Before and after his call the Prophet was personally exposed to Christian influences. His harem included a Christian woman and his household a Christian Syrian slave. Mariya the Copt was the concubine who gave him his only son, who died in infancy; and Zayd ibn-Harithah, the slave, was freed and adopted by Muhammad. Another slave, Bilal, was a Christian Abyssinian who became the first muezzin (*mu'adhdhin*) in Islam.

Besides the religion, the new gospel had social and economic implications that posed a threat to the established order. It would alienate the conservative tribal Arabians from their heathen ancestors and ally them with alien Christians and Jews. Tribal solidarity was then the chief cohesive force in society. The new doctrine would, additionally, undermine the usefulness of the Kaabah as an object of pilgrimage and, next to the caravan, a main source of income. The Kaabah's custody was then in the hands of the Umayyad clan headed by abu-Sufyan, a successor of Qusayy. Abu-Sufyan, grandson of Umayyah, was the leading merchant and caravaneer of Mecca. He became personally involved in more than one sense when his daughter married a convert — an unkind cut indeed.

Moreover the new preacher seemed to insist not only on generosity, which was high on the scale of Arabian values, but on the sharing of wealth, as if the needy had a claim on it. In characterizing the pious the Koran included: "Those in whose wealth there is a recognized right for the beggar and the deprived" (70:24–25). Giving alms (*zakah*) to the needy was made obligatory in the Koran on a level with prayer. Once a poor orphan himself, Muhammad maintained a soft spot in his heart for the needy.

The formerly poor and now rich prophet seems to have been sensi-

The motto of Islam in modern decorative script

tized to the malaise of his community, a community in transit from nomadism to urbanism. He deeply felt the gap between the haves and the have nots. As the mercantile class, the Quraysh of Mecca, waxed rich; the rest felt or seemed poor. Not only did the new Prophet perceive the moving society in which he lived but he definitely related himself to it; he not only saw what was wrong with the society as it was but he presented a plan for changing it to what he thought it ought to be. Not content with the diagnosis, he felt called upon by Allah, who opened to him the secrets of heaven, to provide the remedy. The remedy tasted no more agreeable in the second decade of the seventh century than in any decade of the twentieth. That wealth was a trust to be used for the common good was a novel concept that has not yet been fully realized. Muhammad started with the idea of changing the course of an economic development in his community, he ended by changing the course of history.

On the social side the most daring attempt was that of restructuring the Arabian society on a novel basis, that of religion rather than blood. From time immemorial blood kinship — factual or fictitious — was considered the bond of union between members of a family, of a clan, or of a tribe. To replace that generally accepted social cement with faith was indeed a radical innovation; it seemed inconceivable. The formulation of the new doctrine in the Koran took this expression: "Verily the believers are nought but brothers" (49:10). This made of Islam a fraternal order set against the rest of the world.

Other than the dangerous religious and socioeconomic implications of the rising fraternity, there were political ones. These implications the Meccan oligarchy was not slow to discern. Should the upstart succeed in undermining the religio-socioeconomic order of the Meccan society, he would become automatically its political leader. The powers that be, the Umayyads, escalated their opposition as Muhammad attracted more followers, mostly of low social standing. Predictably, the aristocrats and well-to-do found little to attract them. All kinds of brickbats were hurled at him. He was called a liar, a sorcerer and soothsayer, a possessed man. But the effect was the opposite of what was expected. The zeal of the dedicated, consecrated missionary was by no means dampened. His vision was not dimmed and his pursuit of the ideal did not slacken. The war of words then gave way to one of active persecution sending eighty-three of the believing families into voluntary exile in Abyssinia. This was in 615, five years after the Prophet's call. He himself, however, remained in Mecca under the protection of his uncle abu-Talib, who, though an unbeliever, was bound by the clan's honor not to deliver his charge.

The Quraysh then resorted to another stratagem, boycotting the dissident member and his clan, the Hashimid. For about three years no social dealings or business transactions were allowed. The clan was practically quarantined in its quarters. The situation was aggravated by the death of Muhammad's patron-uncle and of his wife, Khadijah, his first and only wife while she lived.

Although a few prominent Qurayshis, like abu-Bakr, 'Umar ibn-al-Khattab, and 'Ali ibn-abi-Talib, later Muhammad's main supporters, were recruited to the new cause about this time, Muhammad must have felt after nine years of opposition and humiliation that he was fighting in Mecca for a hopeless cause. A change of venue seemed necessary. The choice fell on Ta'if.

16

The two cities, closely associated in certain respects and in Muhammad's mind, were considerably unlike. Ta'if perched on a mount 75 miles southeast of Mecca and 5,800 feet above the sea (4,800 above Mecca). Its soil was fertile, its water abundant, and its climate relatively salubrious. It counted among its products fruits, leather, and wine. To many modern travelers it looks like a village of Lebanon .transplanted into the desert. And just as today oil-rich shaykhs of Arabia consider it the height of luxury to own a summer villa in Lebanon so the caravan-rich Meccans looked upon owning a home at Ta'if. Today Ta'if is the summer capital of the Su'udi (Saudi) government. The Koran makes no mention of the city by name but the reference to the "two towns" in surah 43:30 is usually considered to be to Mecca and Ta'if. How long the Prophet sojourned in this city of exile we are not certain, but of his lack of success we are. The people of Ta'if had for patroness al-'Uzza, the most powerful (as the name indicates) of a female trinity styled by Meccans the daughters of Allah. The first confrontation between the newcomer and the leaders of the community, one of whom had a Qurayshi wife, turned out to be the last. "I would tear to pieces the curtain of the Kaabah," shouted one, "if Allah were to send a one like you." Another asked, "Could not Allah have found anyone else to send but you?" A third remarked, "By Allah, I shall never talk to you. For if you are a messenger from Allah — as you claim to be — you are too important for me to discourse with, and if you are lying against Allah, then I should not discourse with you either."[1]

Words were followed by action. An infuriated mob chased the visitor and pelted him with stones. There was nothing else he could do. He wiped the Ta'if dust off his feet and turned his face Mecca-ward. As he went, the disappointed but not discouraged prophet recited a psalm, Davidian in its beauty, preserved for us by his biographer ibn-Hisham. It began with:

> O Lord, unto Thee do I complain of my helplessness,
> paucity of resourcefulness, and insignificance vis-à-vis
> other men. O most merciful of the merciful. Thou art
> the lord of the helpless and Thou are my lord.

1. Ibn-Hisham, *Sirah,* ed., Ferdinand Wüstenfeld (Göttingen, 1858–1860), p. 280; for a more literal translation see Alfred Guillaume, tr., *The Life of Muhammad* (London, 1955), p. 192.

MECCA

It ended with:

> May it never be that I should incur Thy anger or fail
> to satisfy Thee. For there is no resource or power
> save in Thee.[2]

Before daring to make a public appearance in Mecca, the returning son hid in the Hira' cave for a few days. The protector or sponsor he sought was not forthcoming. Many were approached and none responded. A new kind of audience was felt necessary, and the disappointed persistent preacher thought he could find it among tribesmen and Bedouins frequenting the fairs. He then, to borrow the words of his biographer, went from one fair to another "offering himself" as the messenger of Allah. Fairs (Ar. sing. *suq*), in those days of undeveloped means of communication and limited opportunities for exchange of commodities, loomed high in economic and social importance. They were held in one of the four months of holy truce, during which a moratorium on raids and wars was enforced. They attracted not only merchants from cities and Bedouins from deserts, but poets who recited their latest productions in a sort of contest, horsemen who engaged in tournaments, and others who exhibited their feats. Mecca, in common with other cities, had its fairs.

It was on one of these fair visits that Muhammad in 620 met tribesmen from Yathrib (250 miles north of Mecca) who seemed interested enough to listen. Their city was known to Muhammad through some connection which his mother had. The city had Jewish colonies and the Jews' expectancy of a prophet or Messiah may have favorably predisposed their fellow citizens to the acceptance of an Arabian prophet. The first meeting prepared the way to a later one in which a formal agreement was reached with a delegation of some seventy Yathribis. The Yathribis declared their acceptance of Islam and promised protection in their town to its Prophet and followers — a breakthrough after twelve years of unrewarding effort on the Prophet's part. The migration to Yathrib was carried out with complete secrecy to avert the interference of the Quraysh. The bulk of the old believers, about two hundred, closed their homes and silently stole away. The leader, accompanied by his father-in-law abu-Bakr and his cousin 'Ali, followed, arriving safely at their destination on September 24, 622. This

2. *Ibid.*

migration (*hijrah*, hegira) was chosen later by a successor (*khalifah*, caliph) of Muhammad as the starting point in the new Moslem calendar. It marks the end of the pre-Islamic period. The hijrah split history into two just as the birth of Christ had done.

IV

With the Prophet's departure the spotlight that was shining on Mecca shifted its focus. Yathrib became al-Madinah (in full, Madinat al-Nabi, the City of the Prophet, Medina). Mecca did not yield easily. An eight-year struggle for supremacy ended with victory for the northern rival. After Mecca's surrender to the Prophet (630), Medina was chosen for his residence and the seat of government. His four successors, the Orthodox caliphs (632–661), generally followed his example.

Mecca's surrender meant its acceptance of Islam. The Quraysh, its bitterest foes, now became its staunchest supporters. One after the other of them moved on to the new capital to share in the promotion of the new faith and to embark on new careers. The highest positions in the government and the army were open to them. Many Qurayshis took part in the campaigns that in the Orthodox period, particularly under 'Umar ibn-al-Khattab (634–644), resulted in the conquest of the Fertile Crescent, Persia, and Egypt. Later some served as governors of provinces in the newly acquired domain. Life in Mecca then developed along two opposite lines, one of revelry and the other of piety.

In the wake of the conquests, booty, tribute, and taxes found their way in abundance into the city; they became its new source of income. This more than compensated for the loss of caravan trade. Pilgrimage, of course, continued; in fact it increased. To the city many of its old sons, now retired generals, governors, and other high officials, would return to spend their newly acquired fortunes in ease and comfort, as if in a state of reaction against their past strenuous days. Their sons began where the fathers ended. Once a center of commerce, Mecca now became a center of pleasure. Its *nouveaux riches* brought along harem, dancers, and singers, male and female, as well as new concepts of what constitutes the good life. They lived in baronial style in villas and surroundings the like of which Mecca had never seen before.

The life of pleasure was personified in a Meccan poet, a Qurayshi named 'Umar ibn-abi-Rabi'ah. 'Umar proved that the widely known

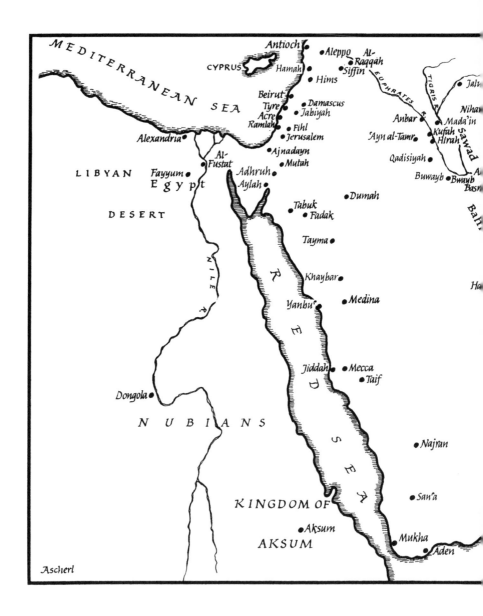

The Arabian Peninsula at the time of Muhammad, ca. 600

saying that the Quraysh excel in everything but poetry was not without an exception. Son of a rich merchant who had served as a governor in Yaman, the charming, lazy beau inherited enough money to enable him to spend his time indulging in drinking, chasing after women, and singing the beauty of fair damsels especially from among visitors. The pilgrim period was his high season. Perfumed, colorfully dressed, and riding a bedecked camel the debonair poet would take his stand where he could view the unveiled ladies — including princesses from the caliphal family in Medina or in Damascus — circumambulating the Kaabah. In refined and tender verse he would describe not only their dresses, movements, and faces but venture into the realm of emotion. 'Umar spent money lavishly to establish contacts with a desired lady. Once he gave a hundred dinars to one who tipped him about the advent of an especially attractive subject. He also used his money for buying slaves and training them to sing and serve his purposes. Set to music his compositions achieved immediate popularity in and beyond the Peninsula; they established his reputation as the one who made Arabic erotic poetry an independent art.

In the meantime Mecca was becoming a rendezvous for pious researchers from all parts of the Moslem world. They sought mementos of the life of the Master, collected traditions about him and his early companions, and compiled data which served as the raw material for his biography and for the early history of Islam. Caliphs expressed their piety by lavish expenditure on buildings and endowments, adding to the parasitic trend among the population. The holy sanctuary, al-Masjid al-Haram, was naturally the chief beneficiary. Its history is interwoven with that of the city. Originally it consisted of the Kaabah, Zamzam, and the traditional place where Abraham stood (*maqam*, station) as he built the Kaabah. When Muhammad in 630 made his triumphal entry into the city, he made of this triple compound a mosque of which the Kaabah remained its holy of holies. Not long after his death the place became inadequate for the needs of worshipers and was enlarged by his second successor 'Umar at the expense of adjacent houses. As the edifice was enlarged it was embellished. The third 'Abbasid caliph al-Mahdi (d. 785) added the colonnades. His son Harun al-Rashid (786–809) made nine visits to Mecca in which he spent money profusely. On one occasion his wife Zubaydah, we are

The holy Kaabah bearing the cover with Koranic inscriptions holds the black
stone in its corner. The dome to the right marks the site of Zamzam

Courtesy Ministry of Information, Riyad

told, expended three million dinars, part of which was used for supplying the city with water from a spring twelve miles away. The source
is still known by her name. The Palestinian geographer al-Maqdisi,
who visited Mecca in the mid–tenth century, saw both shutters of the
Kaabah's door plated with silver coated with gold. The last caliph to
make the sanctuary an object of his interest was the Ottoman sultan
Salim II (d. 1574), to whom it owes its present form.

On the political side Mecca achieved no distinction of which it could
be proud. Its history is punctuated with unsuccessful uprisings against
the established order. The most dangerous and frequent of these were
led by descendants of the fourth caliph, 'Ali ibn-abi-Talib (656–661),
son-in-law of the Prophet and father of al-Hasan and al-Husayn. 'Ali
lost the caliphate to Mu'awiyah (661–680), founder of the Damascus
Umayyad dynasty, a dynasty of usurpers in 'Alid eyes. Equally illegiti-
mate to the 'Alids was the 'Abbasid caliphate in Baghdad. The decline

of the 'Abbasids, however, beginning in the mid–ninth century, threw the outlying parts of the domain into an anarchy and encouraged dissident uprisings. A subversive heterodoxy named Qarmati (after its founder Qarmat, fl. 890, an Iraqi peasant) established a state in the Persian Gulf area and carried ruthless raids into neighboring lands. It did not spare pilgrims to the Holy Cities. Its atrocities culminated in 930, when 1,500 followers pillaged Mecca and carried off the Black Stone, an unheard-of act of heresy. The sacred relic was kept twenty years in captivity and was returned upon payment of a heavy ransom. Only once before had the Highly Honored city been so dishonored. That was in 683 when a Syrian army was sent by Mu'awiyah's son Yazid against the caliphal claimant 'Abdullah ibn-al-Zubayr. The rebel sought sanctuary on the inviolable soil of the sanctuary, but was nevertheless attacked and the Kaabah caught fire. The Black Stone was split in three pieces. The house of Allah, in the words of the great historian al-Tabari, "looked like the torn bosom of a mourning woman."

Mecca experienced other periods of trouble brought about by nature. The sterility of its soil and its high temperature, ranging from 115°F. to 135°F., have been the main troublemakers. Rain is rare and showers are far between, causing periods of drought. With drought went famine. Occasionally, however, heavy rainfalls or violent cloudbursts over the adjoining hills would bring about floods that converted streets into streams and threatened the Kaabah. Chroniclers devote chapters to the floods of Mecca, in whose wake epidemics often spread.

The weakening of the central authority in Baghdad and the mushrooming of petty states gave the city and its 'Alids their chance. In 960 a descendant of al-Hasan (hence his title *sharif*, nobleman) succeeded in establishing an independent rule over the city and its immediate environs. The Hasanid sharifate, with many changes of fortune, endured till well into the twentieth century. For the first three centuries it was virtually independent. The last sharif was Husayn ibn-'Ali, who in 1916 declared himself king of the Arabs and later — when Mustafa Kemal destroyed the Ottoman caliphate — caliph of the Moslems. In 1924–1925 'Abd-al-'Aziz ibn-Su'ud, leader of the Wahhabis of Najd, destroyed the sharifate and added Hijaz to his rising kingdom. Husayn's two sons founded the two kingdoms of Iraq (destroyed in 1958) and that of Jordan.

V

Throughout the vicissitudes of time Mecca's hold on the affections of believers has remained secure. The treatment of the city by geographers, historians, and travelers has invariably been more romantic than objective. Following is a sample from Yaqut al-Rumi (d. 1229), considered the outstanding East Moslem geographer and author of the standard geographical dictionary of Islam:

Thus did the Prophet address Mecca: "By Allah, you are the best of all places on Allah's land and the dearest to me. Had I not been forced out, I would never have left you." . . . He further said, "He who endures patiently Mecca's heat will keep away from him a hundred years of Hell fire, and will draw closer to him two hundred years of Paradise." On a stone found in Mecca an inscription read: "Verily, I the lord of Bakkah the Holy have created it on the day I created the sun and the moon. . . ." As for a description of Mecca: The city lies in a valley, surrounded by mountains on all sides. It is built around the Kaabah with polished black and white stones topped by dried bricks. Several structures have wings of teak wood. Many-storied and white-painted, the houses look attractive. True, the city is hot in summer but its nights are agreeable. Thus did Allah spare its people the burden and the expense of building fires to keep warm in winters. . . . The Kaabah lies in the center of the Mosque. Mecca has no running water; all its water falls from heaven. Nor does it have wells with drinking water. Only the Zamzam water is drinkable and even that cannot be used all the time. In all Mecca there are no fruit trees; the only trees are those of the desert.[3]

The celebrated Spanish-Arab geographer and traveler ibn-Jubayr visited Mecca in August 1183 and devoted a chapter to the exclusive favors and blessings Allah bestowed on it.

The blessed city and its people have ever been the beneficiaries of the prayers of Abraham, Allah's friend — blessing and peace be on him — as revealed by Allah, mighty and majestic is He: "Our Lord, I have made some of my seed dwell in a valley with no sown land by Thy Holy House [Kaabah] so that, O Lord, they may perform prayer. Make then some hearts of men turn to them and make provision of food for them, haply they may be thankful."[4]

3. Yaqut, *Kitab Mu'jam al-Buldan*, ed. Ferdinand Wüstenfeld (Leipzig, 1869; reprint Teheran, 1965), vol. IV, pp. 619, 625–626.

4. Sur. 14:40.

Allah has further declared: "Have We not established for them a safe sanctuary to which all kinds of fruit are brought?"[5] The effect thereof is manifest in the city and shall so continue to the day of resurrection. Indeed men's hearts have not ceased to turn toward the city from distant lands and remote regions. The road to it has been the meeting place of those coming and going from among the recipients of the noble message [of Islam]. Fruits from all lands are brought there too, making it the most favored territory in fruits, utilities, revenue, and trade.

Even if Mecca had no source of income other than the pilgrim season, it would suffice. For in it congregate peoples from the East and the West. Indeed only one day's sale (to-say nothing about other days) of precious treasures — such as pearls, sapphires, and other stones; of perfumes — such as musk, camphor, amber, and aloes; of drugs and other imports of India and Abyssinia; of varied products of Iraq and Yaman; of varied commodities from Khurasan; of goods from al-Maghrib [Morocco] and so on to what cannot be enumerated or limited, was spread over the entire country, it could render brisk all its markets and its benefit would accrue to all of them.

Ibn-Jubayr goes on to discuss the variety of fruits, vegetables, meats, and other foods found at the pilgrim season in Mecca, all of which are the choicest of their kind. He closes the chapter with the following:

There is something marvelous about the blessed water of Zamzam. If drunk from the pit it tastes warm like milk from a camel's udder. In this is evidence of the special care of Allah, extolled is He, whose blessings are too well known to be described. . . . A common experience relates to this blessed water. Whenever one feels worn out with tired muscles — either as a result of circumambulating the Kaabah, performing the minor pilgrimage on foot, or because of any one of the other activities that overtax the. body — and pours this water on his body, he instantly feels relief and vigor and gets rid of what had afflicted him.[6]

On one of his visits to Medina between 1325 and 1354 the Moroccan world traveler ibn-Battutah made friends with several sojourning scholars.

One of them was the righteous and meritorious Shaykh abu-al-'Abbas Ahmad ibn-Muhammad ibn-Marzuq [from Tilimsan], a man given to devotional exercises, fasting and prayer in the Mosque of Allah's Mes-

---

5. Sur. 28:57.

6. Ibn-Jubayr, *Rihlah* (Beirut, 1964), pp. 96–101; for a more literal translation see R. J. C. Broadhurst, *The Travels of Ibn Jubayr* (London, 1952), pp. 116–128.

senger (Allah's blessing and peace be upon him in abundance). The shaykh accepted with resignation all troubles of life in expectation of heavenly reward. He often sojourned in Mecca the venerated, where I met him in the year 28 [728, A.D. 1328–1329]. I found him most assiduous in circumambulating the Kaabah. I marveled at his persistence in doing it despite the excessive heat on the black stone-pavement which under the sun felt like red-hot plates. I have seen water-carriers pour water on it, but no sooner did the water flow beyond the point touched than that spot turned again aglow. Most circumambulators on such days wore sandals, but not abu-al-'Abbas ibn-Marzuq. He would go barefoot.

One day I saw him circuiting, and it occurred to me to accompany him. But no sooner had I reached the pavement and made to the Black Stone for the kiss than I felt the blaze of the stones and resolved to return after the kiss. With great effort, however, I reached the Stone and turned back without completing the circuit. As I walked back I kept spreading my mantle on the ground and stepping on it till I reached the colonnade.[7]

VI

Medieval Europeans knew something about South Arabia, the land of spices and incense, from classical sources which early modern Europeans forgot. Europeans of neither period knew much about Hijaz. The main reason was the koranic curtain lowered in a revelation that read: "O ye who believe, the polytheists only are unclean. Let them not then after this year come near the Sacred Mosque. And if ye fear poverty [by loss of income from visitors] Allah shall reward you from His bounty if He willeth. Lo! Allah is the knower the wise" (9:28). The precise meaning of the verse is not clear, but its interpretation by the theologians left no doubt about the meaning. No non-Moslem is allowed to step on the inviolable soil of Mecca at any time, and the blood of him who ventures is legitimate game. Somehow the forbidden sign over Mecca's door was magnified to include not only Medina but a considerable portion of Hijaz. But while it deterred many, the mystery behind it attracted a few. The curiosity aroused was scientific as well as adventurous. No fewer than twenty-five Italian, Spanish, Swiss, English, and other Christian-born Europeans penetrated the curtain

7. C. Defrémery and B. R. Sanguinetti, *Voyages d'Ibn Batoutah*, Arabic text (Paris, 1893), vol. I, pp. 280–281. For a more literal translation see H. A. R. Gibb, *The Travels of Ibn Battuta* (Cambridge, 1958), vol. I, pp. 175–176.

and lived to make a record. As for those who did not survive, their number cannot be ascertained. Success was conditioned by proficiency in a complicated ritual, familiarity with the minutiae of a system of etiquette, and — what was most difficult — mastery over a language rich in gutturals and laryngeals. A slip anywhere along the line, unless backed by presence of mind and cool courage, might cost an adventurer his life.

The first to venture into the lion's den of Islam was a Bolognese named Ludovico di Varthema. In Damascus, where he made his start to learn the "Moorish language," Varthema adopted Islam, assumed the name Yunis (Jonah), and managed through bribery to enroll himself in the Mamluk garrison. The Mamluk captain was himself a Christian renegade. This was in 1503 when the Mamluk dynasty ruled over Egypt and Syria. When the pilgrimage time came Yunis was given a post in the caravan as an escort. The caravan, which he claimed comprised 40,000 (!) men, arrived at Mecca May 22. After going through the pilgrimage rites with his fellow caravaneers, he lingered in the city till June 12. His general impression was not favorable.

The city he saw was unwalled. It housed 6,000 families but its beggars numbered in the tens of thousands. In the streets flocked 15,000 to 20,000 doves, which were said to come from the stock of that dove which spoke to Muhammad in the form of the Holy Spirit. He noted that God must have cursed rather than blessed the city, for its land produced neither grass nor trees nor anything else.

Clearly Varthema's desire for knowledge lacked the element of accuracy. But considering that he had no predecessors and no knowledge of the literature on the subject, the credibility gap is not surprising. Nevertheless, his brief *Itinerary*, published in Italian at Rome in 1510, was an instant success and passed through a number of editions in the original as well as in its translated versions. It gave its readers the first glimpse of the cradle of Islam and served as a source for later explorers.

More learned than the Italian Varthema was the Spanish Badia y Leblich, a student of medicine, astronomy, botany, and geology as well as a master of Arabic. Badia spent several years in Morocco and Egypt on unknown missions and spent money lavishly from equally unknown sources. Claiming descent from the caliphal 'Abbasid family in Baghdad, he adopted the name 'Ali Bey al-'Abbasi. If he was a Jew,

John L. Burckhardt, *Travels in Arabia* (London, 1829)

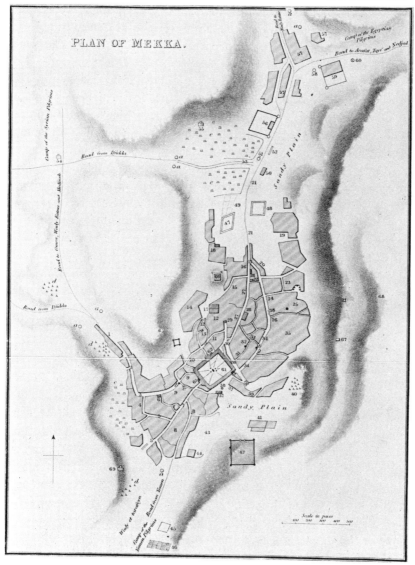

Plan of Mecca, 1814 (Haram Mosque is 61)

as claimed by some, his knowledge of Hebrew must have helped in Arabic pronunciation. With a retinue of servants and an ornamented rug-furnished tent, the princely pilgrim joined the Egyptian caravan arriving in Mecca January 23, 1807. So complete was his disguise that none ever suspected his nationality. Even the sharif of the city be-friended 'Ali Bey and on one occasion sought his assistance in washing the Kaabah's marble floor — a privilege accorded no other Christian-born Westerner.

Badia reports in his *Voyages* that he found no physicians "properly so called" at Mecca and no venders of drugs or medicines. When an inhabitant was sick, his barber bled him, gave him a dose of ginger water, and administered to him some of the Zamzam miraculous water. In describing the different animals he reports lengthily on the bold mice which danced and leapt upon him every night as he slept on the floor. One flower only he saw in all Mecca, but his servant was forbidden to cut it for him for that was sinful. One scientific contribu-tion Badia made was the determination by astronomical instruments of the exact position of the city. Badia's plan of the Haram Mosque, the first of its kind, is remarkably accurate.

It was not the Spaniard's book though that laid the basis of modern exact knowledge of the Holy City but that of a Swiss who followed. John Lewis Burckhardt prepared himself for the perilous task at Aleppo, where he acquired proficiency not only in Arabic but in the sciences of the Koran. Unlike his predecessors he joined no caravan. In mid-July 1814 he entered Jiddah disguised as a beggar in rags. His name was Shaykh Ibrahim ibn-'Abdullah. The following three months he spent in the area, visiting Mecca twice and carrying on researches that gave the minutest details about all ceremonies connected with the pilgrimage. His description of the Mosque remains a classic. To him the city looked like a handsome, albeit decadent town, 3,500 paces in length, with unpaved but broad streets to facilitate pilgrim move-ments. It is the only place in the world where the believer can turn during his prayers to any point of the compass. The houses were lofty, each with a terrace for the harem. Refuse from the windows accumu-lated in the streets. Streets were totally dark at night, but the Mosque was illumined by thousands of lamps. The city, a paradise for beg-gars, was inhabited mostly by people of foreign origin who came as pilgrims and remained. Its entire population numbered 25,000 to 30,000.

England has produced the largest number of world-renowned travelers in Arabia, beginning with Richard F. Burton and coming down to St.

Snouk Hurgronje, *Mekka Bilder-Atlas* (The Hague, 1889)

View of Mecca with Haram Mosque in foreground, 1885

John Philby. Certain accounts of theirs, like *Arabia Deserta* by Charles Doughty and *Seven Pillars of Wisdom* by T. E. Lawrence, have achieved the rank of classics in English literature. Burton started the study of Arabic in Oxford without the benefit of a master and continued it in India, where he served for several years in the East India Company. In 1853 the Royal Geographical Society approved his trip to Africa to explore that "huge white blot" on the map of Arabia. Assuming the name of Shaykh 'Abdullah he posed as a Pathan (Afghani) Indian Moslem to explain his foreign Arabic accent. Burton, the best known among these explorers, did not add much by way of geographic or scientific knowledge to what his forerunners, particularly Badia and Burckhardt, had contributed. But his pungent style, vivid characterization, and the injection of the personal element rendered his works more readable. In his *Personal Narrative of a Pilgrimage to el-Medinah and Meccah* (3 vols., London, 1855–1856) he threw new

31

light on varied aspects of Arabian life. As an author, however, Burton owes his fame more to his translation of the *Arabian Nights*.

Birthplace of the Prophet and the scene of his first revelation, cradle of Islam and the point toward which its adherents turn their faces daily in prayer and direct their feet annually in pilgrimage, Makkah al-Mukarramah is the holiest place in Islam and one of the holiest in the world.

2

Medina:
The Caliphal Capital

O Lord, Thou hast taken me out of a place dearest unto me;
take me now to a place dearest unto Thee.

Muhammad in a tradition

South Arabians named it Yathrib. Pre-Islamic North Arabians had no other name for it. Ptolemy's geography, written in the mid–second Christian century, makes the name Iathrippa. Stephen of Byzantium (flourished first half of sixth century) uses the same form in his geographical dictionary. Yathrib had no history. It had to wait until its name was changed to Madinat al-Nabi (the City of the Prophet, shortened to al-Madinah, anglicized Medina) — more specifically until that day of September 24, 622, when Muhammad set foot on its soil. Aramaic has the same term for city as the Arabic, and the Aramaic-speaking Jews in the neighborhood may have used it for Yathrib.

Medina sharply differed from Mecca. It was an oasis, 2,095 feet above the sea, nucleated on fresh-water wells. The Tropic of Cancer, passing between it and Mecca, consigns it to the temperate zone. The city was then and is still today noted for its produce of dates, cereals, and vegetables. Like Mecca, Medina had experienced the tensions and dislocations concomitant on transition from a nomadic to a settled way of life — agricultural rather than mercantile — but unlike Mecca it, at the time of the hijrah, lacked cohesion in its population and unity in its leadership. Its current malaise stemmed from chronic conflict between its two leading tribes, the Aws and the Khazraj — both of

33

South Arabian origin. The situation was complicated by the existence in the settlement of three tribes of foreign origin, Jewish.

I

Muhammad's first urgent problem in his new abode involved, obviously, the feeding and lodging of the two hundred Emigrants (Muhajirun), whose properties in Mecca had been confiscated by the authorities there. The solution was ready-made; it entailed invoking his doctrine of Islam as a religious brotherhood. Accordingly, each one of the Medinese Moslems, now styled Supporters (Ansar), was required to serve as host for one of the Emigrants.

The next step was to forge the Emigrants, the Supporters (to be jointly called later Companions, *Sahabah*), and their followers into a new unit whose members stand one for the other and all against the world — of course, under his leadership. Presumably more than one pact was concluded, aiming at establishing internal peace and security with the provision that all disputes be settled among the members or be referred to Muhammad. Even if the aggressor be a member's son, the group should act as one against him. Among the followers, the Jews, hitherto the financiers of the town, would so remain, with the difference that hereafter they would acknowledge Muhammad's headship and contribute to the war chest. In return they would receive protection as well as fair treatment. This so-called constitution of Medina was more political than religious. Following are excerpts from an evidently telescoped version in Muhammad's biography:

In the name of Allah, the merciful, the compassionate. This is a document written by Muhammad the Prophet establishing the relations between the believers and Moslems of the Quraysh [Mecca] and of Yathrib, together with those who followed them, joined them and struggled with them. They are all now one community (*ummah*) to the exclusion of all other people. . . . A believer shall not kill another believer for the sake of an unbeliever, nor shall he aid an unbeliever against a believer. . . . For verily the believers are friends one to the other to the exclusion of all others. . . .

It shall not be lawful to a believer who acknowledges this document and believes in Allah and the last day to aid or shelter an innovator [dissident]. And he who offers aid or shelter, Allah's curse and anger shall be on him on the day of resurrection. Neither repentance nor

View of Medina with the Prophet's Mosque, 1969

ransom shall be accepted from him [he is outlawed]. Whenever you disagree on a matter, that matter should be referred to Allah and to Muhammad, peace be upon him. As for the Jews, they shall contribute to war expenses so long as they are fighting alongside the believers.[1]

The terms of this agreement leave no doubt about Muhammad's ability to negotiate, conciliate, and ultimately dominate. Its signing can be said to mark the birth of the community of Islam (*ummat al-Islam*). Hitherto the tribe was the community, hereafter the federation of tribes bound by religion was to be the community. Starting as a partnership between Meccan and Medinese Moslems and their followers, the small band of early believers, the community of Islam in Medina, became a miniature of the universal Islam to be.

1. Ibn-Hisham, pp. 341–342; for a more literal translation see Guillaume, pp. 232–233.

MEDINA

With his position seemingly consolidated in his city of migration, Muhammad turned his attention to the city of his nativity. Mecca had a mystique of its own. It was a center of worship before it became a center of trade. Its tradition was one of holiness. Its Quraysh were peerless as custodians of a national shrine, controllers of international trade, and consummate politicians. No, not Medina but Mecca was to be the radiant center of Islam and its religious capital.

So long as Muhammad was in Mecca, he was on the defensive. His attitude was conciliatory; his approach basically religious. But now the situation radically changed. His attitude became hostile and his approach politico-military. "Subdue and convert" was the new motto, of which a better version would read: subdue and conversion will follow.

The first armed conflict had for aim the interruption of the Meccan caravan on its way back from Syria. Such a blow, if effective, would not only impair the life line of the enemy city but would, with the acquired booty, bolster the tottering economy of the host city. For battlefield, Badr, a watering place on the caravan route southwest of Medina was chosen. The date was mid-March 624. With some three hundred men Muhammad inflicted a humiliating defeat on a host more than three times its number led by abu-Sufyan, shaykh of Quraysh. There was no doubt about it: the victory was a vindication of the faith. More concrete evidence was provided by the fact that thousands of angels participated in the fight as reported in the Koran 8:9–12, 17; 3:120. The fact that twelve months later the Meccans, again under abu-Sufyan, won a battle at Uhud, a short distance north of Medina, and even inflicted two or three wounds on the Prophet's face and leg did not dim the luster of the preceding encounter. At Badr, Islam the religion took on a new dimension, a military one. It embarked on a career that did not end until its flag waved triumphantly over a large part of the civilized world.

Another attempt was necessary to convince the Quraysh of the futility of their effort. In 627 a host of 10,000 Meccans, Bedouins, Jews, and Abyssinians (many of them mercenaries) marched against the rival city and laid siege to it. The combination was styled the "confederates" (ahzab) in the Koran (sur. 33). Muhammad could muster only 3,000. In vain did the besiegers' cavalry try to cross the trenches extemporaneously dug around the city. The withdrawal after a month

Arcade of Prophet's Mosque, Medina

was complete. Never again was Meccan heathenism to measure swords with Medinese Islam.

The Jewish contingent was manned by recruits from Khaybar, an oasis a hundred miles north of Medina, and by Medinese Jews expelled by Muhammad subsequent to the battle of Uhud. That was the second expulsion, the first having taken place after Badr. All Jewish property in Medina was on both occasions confiscated — an Allahsend to the needy community of Islam. Khaybar's turn came now. The Jewish tribe of Khaybar, as intransigent as their coreligionists in Medina, had made of their oasis a stronghold considered impregnable against

37

Bedouin attack, but the new attack was of a different kind. After a two-week assault ending June 628, the settlement yielded and was rendered innocuous. It agreed to give half of its produce of the land to the victor and live in peace under his protection. The Jewish-Arabian problem was solved.

The Koran favors the Jews, in common with the Christians, with the designation "people of the Book." That made them sharers with Moslems of the privilege of being depositories of revealed scriptures, with the difference that the Koran was in perspicuous Arabic (6:59; 16:105; 26:29; 43:1–2). Muhammad thereby gained for his new religion old-age respectability. Throughout the pre-hijrah period, the relations between the two parties were cordial, both agreeing on the fundamentals of belief. But it was not long after Muhammad's landing in Medina before his hopes of integrating the local Jews into his community were dashed. As the "chosen people of Jehovah" the Jews considered themselves unique. They could accept no Messiah who was not of the seed of Abraham. In his second year at Medina, Jerusalem, the kiblah since pre-hijrah days, was by revelation superseded by Mecca (2:139, 144). The muezzin's voice was substituted for the gong, and Friday was designated as the day for the congregational prayer featuring the sermon. Jews were charged with having falsified the scriptures by concealment, corruption, and forgery (2:169; 4:48; 5:16). Their liquidation became a necessity. As for the rest of the people of the Book, their being no Christian settlement in either Mecca or Medina, the opportunities for parallel deterioration in relations with Islam were nil. But the Christians, too, had falsified the scriptures. Muhammad's reaction was the first step to disassociate Islam from its two sister monotheistic religions and to Arabianize it.

Throughout the post-hijrah period the Prophet did not cease to receive revelations but they were of a different substance and style. Whereas those of Mecca were basically religious, expressed in incisive terms and in rhythmic, rhymic style, the revelations of Medina were prosaic and verbose dealing with such subjects as marriage and divorce, heredity and orphanage, food and drink, war and peace — all reflecting the changed conditions.

By early 630 the Prophet had felt so secure as to make the holy pilgrimage to the Mecca sanctuary, the first one since his hijrah. At the head of a thousand followers he made his triumphal entry into the city without striking a blow. He made his way straight into the Kaabah, smashed the hundreds of idols therein, and accepted the conversion of his enemies, even their leader abu-Sufyan. Of the general amnesty he declared, only ten were excepted and proscribed. He certainly knew how to be magnanimous in his victory, as he knew how to be resolute and unnerved in his defeat. After a sojourn of three months he returned to his seat at Medina. By then the reputation of the Prince-Prophet had spread beyond the confines of Hijaz. Tribal delegations flocked from all quarters offering homage and alms-tax (*zakah*). A principal obligation of Islam, zakah served as a symbol of submission and as a contribution to the needy of the new community. Among the delegations was one from Christian Najran, marking the first triumph of Islam over Christianity.

Amidst preparations for expeditions into southern Palestine, where further opportunities for contact with Christendom awaited, Muhammad was taken ill of fever (typhoid?) and died June 8, 632.

II

Arabia is one of those rare countries that can boast two cities that were and remained great throughout their history. Twelve years of Muhammad in Mecca (610–622) gave Mecca its permanent claim on greatness. Ten years of his life in Medina (622–632) plus the twenty-nine years of the residence of his immediate successors, the Orthodox caliphs (632–661), constitute Medina's claim. The two cities have not ceased to exercise their fascination over men and women the world over and to attract thousands of them for a visit.

Muhammad's caliphs succeeded him in his functions as head of the state, commander of the army, and chief justice but not as a prophet. For he, as the last (*khatam*, seal, sur. 33:40) of the prophets, could have no successor. Not only does his dispensation supersede all earlier ones but it is in itself perfect and final, fit for all time and all places. The caliphate, therefore, was not fully a theocracy. The government of the state was not by the immediate direction of Allah, nor was it by priests as representatives of Allah. Islam had no priesthood; it was a lay religion, and the caliph was not a pope. He led in the congregational prayer and delivered the Friday sermon, but both were functions any humble citizen could perform. As commander in chief of the armed forces, Muhammad's successor included, among his duties, protection and promotion of the faith and enforcing the divine law.

The four Orthodox (*rashidun*, rightly guided) caliphs — abu-Bakr, 'Umar, 'Uthman and 'Ali — were so called because supposedly they conducted their offices under the inspiration of the Prophet's precept, example, and personality, so closely related were they to him not only by blood kinship but by faith and labor. All four were Qurayshis; all were early believers, friends, and collaborators. Their capital was Medina and their era extended from 632 to 661. Their rule was patriarchal and tribal, rather than monarchic or imperial, and their domestic lives almost throughout were simple and unostentatious. Piety featured their daily conduct.

The principal events enacted in Medina under the Orthodox caliphate can be summed up under four headings: the Islamization of the Peninsula, the canonization of the Koran, the conquest of the Fertile Crescent, Persia, and Egypt, and the civil war. Islamization and conquest went to a certain extent hand in hand now and later. In the case of the bulk of Arabia both were the proud achievement of the first caliph abu-Bakr (632–634), father-in-law of the Prophet and a former merchant. At the death of Muhammad several tribes and communities withheld the payment of zakah, implying secession from Islam. The law in such cases is clear: Once a Moslem always a Moslem. Apostasy is punishable by death (sur. 16:108). But this was more than apostasy. It had political aspects — including resentment against Medina's sudden hegemony — as well as economic aspects, involving payment of tax. This was the first crisis confronting the nascent state. As they seceded, tribes declared for false prophets. The sixty-year-old caliph was unrelenting in his determination to crush all uprisings and to return dissidents into the fold, and having done that, he proceeded to accomplish the conquest of the rest of the Peninsula. Unless the Peninsula conquered and Islamized itself, how could it conquer and Islamize the outside world?

That all Arabia had in Muhammad's lifetime embraced Islam — as Arab chroniclers assert — is difficult to believe in view of the short time involved and the primitive means of communication. Even Mecca did not submit until two years before the Prophet's death. Writing a hundred years or more after the events the chroniclers viewed them from the wrong perspective. Not the Prophet but his first successor consolidated the power of the faith south as far as Hadramawt and 'Uman, and east to the Persian Gulf. For the first time in its history the Peninsula was seemingly united under one scepter and subjected to one prophet. One of the generals who contributed to that end was a brilliant Qurayshi, Khalid ibn-al-Walid. Khalid had started his military career on the battlefields of Badr and Uhud against Muhammad; he was to end it on the battlefields of northern Syria and to earn the unique title of "the sword of Allah."

As the Book of Allah, the Koran, complete and ready, existed from eternity, but was dictated piecemeal to Muhammad in the course of twenty-two years beginning 610. Revelations were occasioned by particular conditions confronting the Prophet partly in Mecca, mostly in Medina. During his lifetime Muhammad does not seem to have attempted a systematic collection of his revelations and their fixing by committal to writing. Certain undetermined fragments were no doubt recorded by him through his scribe, Zayd ibn-Thabit, who also carried out the correspondence with Jews and others. At the Prophet's death the door of revelation was forever locked.

Tradition credits 'Umar, undoubtedly the best mind among the Orthodox caliphs, with having suggested to his predecessor the compilation and establishment of the koranic text. The suggestion was prompted by the fact of the decimation, by domestic and foreign wars, of those early specialists in koranic study called readers (*qurra'*) and memorizers (*huffaz*). After consulting with Zayd, abu-Bakr hesitated. How could he undertake what the Prophet had not? But other developments forced his hands. Varying readings and versions were already in currency, disputes about the identification of material were rising, and divisions in the ranks of believers threatened. Precisely what was the character of the first caliph's performance modern research has not been able to ascertain. The honor of fixing the Holy Book in its final form was left to his second successor 'Uthman ibn-'Affan (644–656). This must have been about 650.

'Uthman entrusted the delicate task to a committee of Qurayshis chaired by Zayd. The committee collected the material from written records, some of which came from palm leaves, stones, and animal

41

shoulderblades, and from oral records preserved in "breasts of men" (memories). Some early surahs presumably never were recorded, but there is no evidence that the original material suffered from interpolation or deletion. Judging by the finished product no critical editorial work whatever was done. Descriptive, narrative, legislative, and declamatory fragments stand side by side. Textual defects, grammatical difficulties, and confused thoughts are not rare, necessitating an endless series of commentaries, and giving rise to one of the principal sciences of Islam, koranic exegesis. Considering the fact, however, that the Koran was the first piece of written Arabic literature, the surprising thing is that the style is not more troublesome.

The arrangement of the one hundred and fourteen surahs in the book followed no chronological or logical order. The consideration was purely mechanical — the longest first. This put the earliest surahs at the end of the book. The only exception was the first, the opener (*al-fatihah*),[2] a gem of a prayer serving as an introduction. It is supposed to be reiterated by the devout four times with each of the five daily ritual prayers, making it a competitor of the Lord's Prayer. Equally mechanical was the titling of the surahs, achieved by lifting a word, at times haphazardly, from the early part of the surah and using it as a heading. Such is the case of the second surah, longest and richest of all in legislative material, entitled The Cow (*al-baqarah*), though only four verses (63–66) out of two hundred and eighty-six, deal with a cow, that of Moses.

The 'Uthmanic version, being official, became canonical. The mother copy was kept in Medina; three duplicates were sent to Kufah, Basrah, and Damascus, headquarters then of Arabian armies. All copies in circulation since then have presumably been replicas of these originals. The calligrapher undertakes his task as a religious duty. Lithographing is permissible, but not printing. A typographical error is tantamount to a sin. One Islamic heterodoxy, the Khariji, rejected

---

2. In the name of God, the merciful, the compassionate.
   Praise be to God, lord of the universe,
   the merciful, the compassionate,
   ruler on the day of judgment.
   Thee alone we worship, and Thee alone we ask for aid.
   Guide us in the straight path,
   the path of those whom Thou hast favored,
   not of those against whom Thou art wrathful,
   nor of those who go astray.

The opening chapter of the Koran. The text is repeated in the margin
in early eighteenth-century illuminated script

the twelfth surah on the ground that such an amorous affair as that of Joseph and the Egyptian woman could not have been a proper subject for revelations. The Shi'ah allege suppression of certain verses favorable to 'Ali and to 'Ali's family, but the bulk of the Moslem community accepts the authenticity of the koranic text in its present form, and modern scholars agree.

The canon of the Koran contributed inestimably not only to the religious and linguistic but to the political unification of the emerging community of Islam. It provided believers of all varieties with a common ground on which to stand. To abu-Bakr's attempt to unify Moslem Arabians by the sword was now added 'Uthman's attempt to unify all Moslems by the written word.

Muhammad laid the background for Moslem-Arabian expansion and provided the necessary conditions, but he could hardly be said to have initiated it outside the Peninsula. True, before his death he did send his lieutenants on several expeditions northward, reaching Mu'tah near the southern tip of the Dead Sea, but evidently the objective was ensuring control over the Peninsular trade route and establishing contact with Arabian tribes domiciled in that area. It was under his first successor that the aggressive expansionist movement was launched.

The launching was due less to deliberate planning and consultative design than to a socio-economic-religious complex over which the caliph had no full control. The war machine generated by abu-Bakr's generals on the battlefield of the Peninsula acquired momentum that could not be checked. Raids (Ar. *ghazu*, whence razzia) for booty was a time-honored intertribal institution that gave chance to the have nots to share with the haves and could not be totally obliterated by a fiat from a religious fraternity. It sought new channels for its expression. Islam substituted for it the holy war (*jihad*): military action aimed at the expansion of the faith as well as its defense. Theoretically it is the only form of war authorized, leaving no room for such thing as secular war (2:186–190). Jihad sets the community of Islam against the world, paralleling the view of modern communism. As for him who dies in the jihad, he dies in the path of Allah; he stays alive (2:149) and his share in Paradise is immediately assured. Early Arab chroniclers used the same term *ghazu* for the Moslem battles, and the word *fath* (opening, opening the way ultimately for Islam) for conquest. Their interpretation of the phenomenal success did not differ from that of the Hebrews eighteen centuries earlier: providential. Political leaders proclaimed and theologians agreed that the ultimate objective was making the world safe for the religion of Islam. To the hardened sons of the desert the sedentary people of the north must have seemed like effete snobs.

On the other side of the fence internecine wars for over two centuries between the Persians and the Eastern Romans or Byzantines, the two giant powers of the area and era, had come close to destroying their military potential. The Byzantine Empire dominated the Mediterranean basin and sought eastward expansion. The Persian Empire dominated the eastern hinterland and directed its thrust westward. The border states of Syria and Mesopotamia became the battleground. Additionally, both empires were suffering from dynastic troubles. The two incumbents of the thrones had assumed their positions by the use of force against their predecessors. Between 613 and 616 Khusrau II occupied Syria (including Palestine) and Egypt, and the following year added Asia Minor, reaching Chalcedon opposite Constantinople. In 628–629 Heraclius brought to a successful conclusion his campaigns for the restoration of the lost territory, recovered the Holy Cross plundered by the Persians, and amidst great jubilation reinstated it in Jerusalem. One factor played into the hands of the Arabians. Both the eastern borders of Syria and the western borders of Persia were held by Arabian tribes domiciled there for centuries and by now Christianized. They nevertheless felt closer in blood and language to the newcomers. Even in religion they did not feel far removed from Arabian Moslems. In fact one could say that the bulk of the Christian Semitic population of the area had been alienated from their Byzantine masters by taxation and by disabilities under which they labored. Being Jacobites and Nestorians they were regarded as heretics in their Christology by the Orthodox Church of Constantinople. To the natives it was simply a matter of exchange of masters in the hope of a new deal.

The wave of conquest beyond Arabia, set in motion under abu-Bakr, was accelerated by 'Umar (634–644), climaxed under him, and terminated under his successor 'Uthman (644–656). In the rapidity and ease with which it was executed and in the phenomenal success which was achieved, this conquest ranks among the most spectacular in military annals.

Syria, from Sinai to the Taurus, was the first to yield. In all, the operation took about seven years, between 633 and 640. The hero was Khalid ibn-al-Walid. His first major victory was over the Byzantine capital Damascus. The city opened its gates to the besiegers in September 635 after a siege shortened to six months by negotiated agreement on the part of its native bishop and its state treasurer, the father of St. John Damascene, the last great hymnologist and theologian of the Eastern Syrian Church. The second victory worthy of note was also scored by Khalid. It took place eleven months later at the Yarmuk, an eastern tributary of the Jordan River. Here Moslem troops of some 25,000 decisively routed a Byzantine army of almost twice that number comprising Greeks, Armenians, Syrians, and other mercenaries, and accompanied by priests carrying icons and chanting prayers. The battle cry of *Allahu akbar* (God is greatest) proved more effective. The way was open for the subjugation of the entire country. One Syrian city after the other fell as if domino pieces in a row. In the north even such cities as Antioch (Antakiyah) and Laodicea (al-Ladhiqiyah), with Greek names and Greek origins, offered no marked resistance. "The people of Shayzar [near Hamah]," in the words of an early historian of the conquests, "went out to meet the conqueror accompanied by players on the tambourine and singers and bowed down before him."[3] In the south the only city which was stubborn in its defense was Hellenized Caesarea (Qaysariyah). Its position on the sea gave it the advantage of receiving supplies from the Byzantine navy, for which the Arabians had no counterpart. The city finally succumbed (October 640) under an attack led by Mu'awiyah, son of abu-Sufyan, and facilitated by a Jewish leader inside the walls. With the conquest of Syria the first foreign province was added to the emerging caliphal state.

Of special interest are the terms of the treaty signed by Khalid on the eve of his entry into Damascus, modeled on the terms offered by Muhammad to the Christians of Najran. They in turn served as a model for later treaties:

In the name of Allah, the merciful, the compassionate. This is what Khalid ibn-al-Walid would grant the people of Damascus if he enters

3. Philip K. Hitti, *Origins of the Islamic State* (translation of al-Baladhuri, *Futuh al-Buldan*) (New York, 1916; reprint Beirut, 1966), pp. 201–202.

it: He shall give them security for their lives, property, and churches. Their city walls shall not be demolished and no Moslems shall be quartered in their dwellings. Thereunto we give them the pact of Allah together with the protection of His Prophet (Allah's blessing and peace be upon him), of the caliphs and of all believers. So long as they pay poll-tax, nothing but good shall befall them.[4]

The turn of Egypt came next. The invasion was undertaken on the initiative of an officer in the Syrian army, 'Amr ibn-al-'As, and with the half-hearted consent of the caliph 'Umar. For credentials 'Amr offered his knowledge of the terrain — having been a caravaneer on the Hijaz-Egypt road — and his military experience in Syria — having taken part in the siege of Damascus and the battle of the Yarmuk. Like Khalid, he was a Qurayshi who had participated in the battles against the Prophet and did not embrace Islam until shortly before the fall of Mecca in 630.

Starting with 4,000 horsemen 'Amr in December 639 crossed the Syro-Egyptian frontier, crushed all resistance in his way, and bid his time awaiting reinforcement before tackling the strongly fortified citadel Babalyun. Strategically situated on a point at the Nile where Upper and Lower Egypt meet (later site of Cairo), Babalyun had a garrison of 5,000 men, and by the time recruits from Medina had augmented the invading troops to 10,000, the Byzantine army of defense had reached 20,000. Cyrus the governor, who was also the patriarch, offhandedly spurned the offer of Islam or surrender. He chose the only alternative left: the sword. In April 641 the besieged fortress surrendered and the way was open to the capital Alexandria. The march was more like a promenade. The Copts of Egypt followed the Christology of the Syrian Church and had been as badly treated, both politically and religiously, by their Byzantine masters. Alexandria was the next target. Capital of the province, base for the fleet, the city of Alexandria was protected by walls and towers, manned by a garrison of 50,000, and ranked in might and affluence next to the city founded by Constantine. By contrast, the Arabian challengers, with no siege equipment, not a single ship, and far from base, must have looked like a sad lot on that summer day in 642 when they camped outside the high walls. But the will to conquer was on their side and they pressed the assault undismayed. By September 642 the city was

4. *Ibid.*, p. 187.

ready to capitulate. The victorious march continued westward to add Cyrenaica, a Berber territory which, for the time being, constituted the farthest limit of the westward thrust.

The commander in chief now began to function as governor general. For capital 'Amr chose the site where he had pitched his camp outside Babalyun to become known as Fustat (from Gr., meaning camp). One of the first buildings was expectedly the mosque, still standing in what is today Old Cairo. 'Amr utilized the existing Byzantine machinery, administrative and financial, with certain adaptations. He proved to be as brilliant and dashing a soldier as Khalid — who was humiliated and downgraded by 'Umar for acting too independently — but more wily and more capable in administration. When the new caliph 'Uthman wanted to send from Medina a fiscal agent for the new province, 'Amr objected on the ground that that amounted to one man holding the cow's horns and another milking it.

In the meantime not all was quiet on the eastern front. The column that had started from Medina in 632 encountered preliminary difficulties until its command was entrusted to Sa'd ibn-abi-Waqqas, a worthy peer of Khalid and 'Amr. Member of a Meccan family and an early believer, Sa'd had so distinguished himself on the battlefields of Badr and Uhud that he was included by the Prophet among the elite assured of reservations in Paradise. At Qadisiyah to the southwest of Hirah Sa'd at the head of 10,000 had the first chance to measure on a large scale Arabian against Persian swords. Not only did the foe have the advantage in numbers — being almost six times as many — but it included in its equipment war elephants, a novelty in Arabian combat. This was late in the spring of 637. On the advice of a Persian prisoner, the animal enemy was successfully dealt with, the commanding general Rustam fell in battle, and the army dissolved in panic. The victory sealed the fate of Mesopotamia, where the Aramaic-speaking population was no more eager to defend the homeland than their coreligionists in Syria and Egypt. Ctesiphon (Ar. Mada'in), once capital of the Parthian kingdom and now of the Sasanid empire, lay across the Tigris, helpless and hopeless. Deserted by its garrison, its young, inexperienced monarch Yazdajird III fled with his jewels and treasures. But enough was left to dazzle the big black eyes of desert Arabians as they fell upon them, and to overtax the Arabic vocabulary of historians trying to describe the booty. According to one reporter, who had no benefit of a computer, the value reached nine hundred million silver pieces. The muezzin's voice raised in Arabic for the first time atop the palace of the Khusraus has not ceased ever since to reverberate over Persian soil.

Practically all the country now lay at the invader's mercy. Only Nihawand northeast of the capital offered some resistance which was crushed in 641 by a lieutenant of Sa'd. As for the ill-starred Yazdajird, he continued his flight from one hiding place to another till 651 when he was murdered at a miller's hut near Marw by one of his people coveting the crown jewels. Thus came to an ignoble end an empire that had lasted, with some vicissitudes, for twelve hundred years and that was not to rise again for some eight hundred more.

III

'Umar, the strongest and most energetic in the Orthodox series, was succeeded by 'Uthman, the weakest. 'Uthman's reign from 644 to 656 witnessed not only the end of the wave of conquest but the beginning of civil disturbances that did not cease until Medina yielded to Damascus as the mistress of the world of Islam.

Unlike his predecessors the new caliph, a late believer, belonged to the Umayyad aristocracy, lived in relative luxury, favored his relatives with lucrative posts, and thereby aroused the discontent not only of pietists and politicians but of tribesmen in Syria, Egypt, and South Arabia, restless under Medina's mounting centralization of power. The political aspect was complicated by the fact that 'Ali, for long a caliphal aspirant, had by now a sizable following. Disaffection broke into open rebellion, leading to the assassination of the aged caliph in his residence while reading the copy of the Koran he had authorized. His was the first caliphal blood shed by a Moslem. 'Ali was proclaimed as his successor.

Everything seemed to augur well for the new caliph. He was Muhammad's first cousin and husband of his favorite daughter Fatimah; he was first or second male believer and a comrade at arms throughout the Medinese period. His sword was dubbed dhu-al-Faqar, breaker of vertebrae. But there was a fly in the ointment: the possibility of complicity in 'Uthman's murder involving the legitimacy of his rule. The

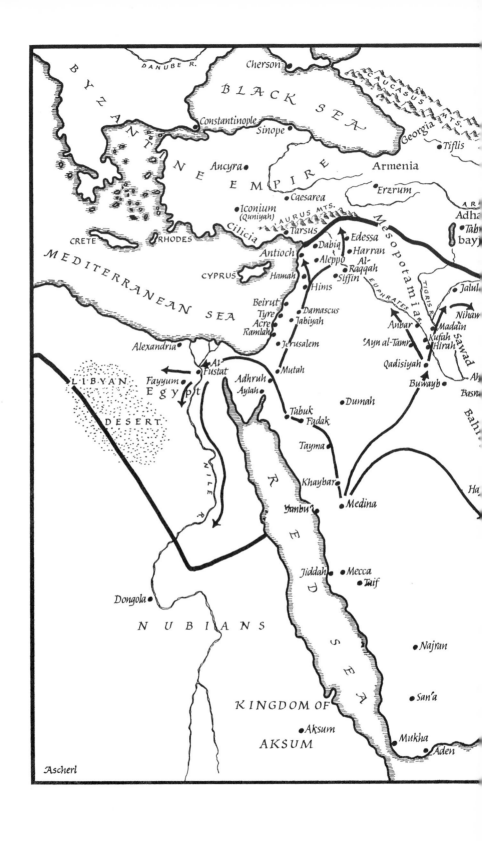

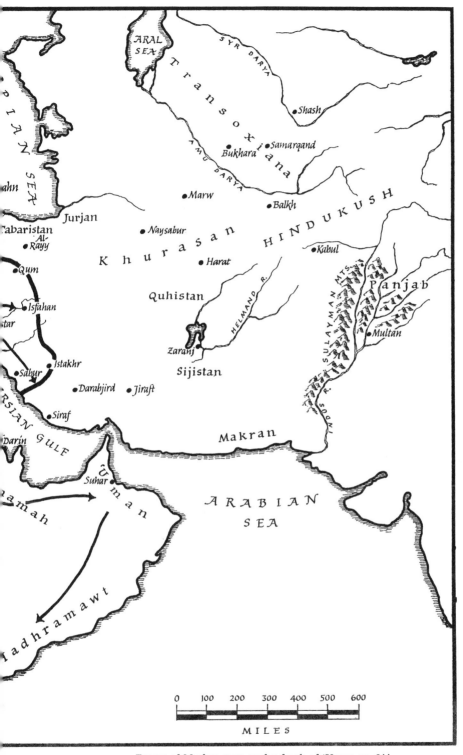

Extent of Moslem state at the death of 'Umar, ca. 644

question was raised by Mu'awiyah, kinsman of the murdered caliph and currently governor of Syria. The shrewd governor withheld his allegiance but did not come forth as a candidate for the highest position in the state. He only wanted 'Ali to bring the culprits before the bar of justice or accept the role of complicity. Even if he could, 'Ali would not; they were his main supporters. As the struggle for power dragged on, Hijaz stood behind its favorite son; and Iraq, for reasons of its own against Syria, did likewise. Syria was solid behind its governor. 'Ali chose Kufah for residence and from it led the mustered Hijazi-Iraqi army to nip the Syrian uprising in the bud. The confrontation took place at Siffin on the western bank of the Euphrates. After days of skirmishing ending July 657, the tide turned in 'Ali's favor and Mu'awiyah resorted to a ruse. He lifted in the air lances with copies of the Koran fastened to their heads, suggesting an appeal to the decision of the Koran from the decision of arms. Against his best judgment the good-hearted caliph agreed. Agreement amounted to arbitration. Arbitration meant lowering his status to that of a pretender and by the same token, raising that of the governor to the same level. As a by-product it alienated some of his staunchest supporters who seceded from the party, were dubbed Kharijis, and, as often happens in such cases, became his bitterest foes. They actively engaged him in fighting for a time. At last on a January 661 Friday, as the caliph was on his way to the Kufah mosque, a Khariji fatally stabbed him with a poisoned sabre. The Kharijis represent the first schism in the body of Islam. They developed their own theology, as did later sects, all of which began as political parties. In Islam one would search in vain for a religious group that did not begin as a political one.

'Ali's removal from the scene cleared the way before his challenger, already declared caliph. Mu'awiyah chose Damascus for capital. Therewith was the curtain lowered on Medina.

IV

Among Arab — one could say Moslem — cities, Medina enjoys the unique distinction of having been both holy and imperial. Its imperialism was lost by the removal of the caliphal seat to Syria; its holiness was never lost. The halo of sanctity, assumed by the one-decade residence of the Prophet, received added luster from his burial in the city

Arcade of the Prophet's Mosque, Medina

and from the mosque he built, the first of its kind. As years rolled by, the pious human memory added to, rather than subtracted from, the luster. Following the example of the Mecca sanctuary, this mosque was declared haram and later the entire city became forbidden area for non-Moslems. A haram area provides protection not only for human beings but for trees, which should not be cut, and birds, which should not be shot. As the second goal of the holy pilgrimage, Medina's sanctity had the opportunity of perennial self-renewal.

No more a rendezvous for politicians and warriors, it became a rendezvous for students and scholars. Some sought spiritual enlightenment and edification, others intellectual enrichment. In competition with Mecca it had the advantage of being heir to a larger share of the legacy of early Islamic piety. Its Companions and the first Medinese believers served as an inexhaustible firsthand source of information. The Mosque functioned as a university. To the would-be theologians, legists, and traditionists a sojourn in Medina was the equivalent of a graduate course nowadays.

The learning of the age was exemplified in Malik ibn-Anas (715–795), theologian, jurisconsult, and traditionist. Malik insisted that the living tradition and agreed practice of his native town be given their due in the formulation of Islamic law. He outlined the first formula of the consensus of public opinion (*ijma'*) as prevalent in Medina. His lectures made him the center of a widening circle of students and admirers. This chief jurist (*imam*) of Medina, as he was honorifically titled, unwittingly lent his name to a school that took its place among the four orthodox schools of law. It spread into Spain and North Africa, where his book *al-Muwatta'* (the levelled path) was used as a text not long after his death. Today the Maliki system prevails in North Africa, Sudan, Nigeria, and eastern Arabia.

At the same time life in Medina, as in Mecca, was developing along a different line, the line of worldliness. After all, the golden stream from the provinces in the form of personal and land tax poured into Medina first. So overwhelming was the volume flooding the state treasury that when the first governor of Bahrain reported to 'Umar the figure 5,000,-000 dirhams, the caliph could not believe him. He asked his governor to "sleep on it" and return. After the Friday congregational prayer, the caliph made the following public announcement: "We have received such an abundance of wealth that we are not sure how to handle. If it is your wish we shall count for each person his share, otherwise we shall weigh it."

The caliph then proceeded to draw a list beginning with the members of the Prophet's family and continuing through the Companions, each to receive a subsidy according to his or her priority in the profession of the faith. Muhammad's favorite widow, 'A'ishah, headed the list with 12,000 dirhams. The average allotment for those who followed was 4,500 dirhams. The minimum stipend for a war veteran amounted to 450 dirhams.

In its bid for the patronage of the new elite of pleasure-seekers, Medina had, over her rival to the south, the advantages of higher altitude, richer water supply, and more extensive gardens. Retired governor officials, civil and military, brought along their slaves and concubines, their singers, dancers, and musicians — male and female — and created an atmosphere never experienced before in the Holy City. At times Medinese engaged, as a pastime, in uprisings against the establishment in Damascus or Baghdad. On one such occasion (in 747) the Umayyad caliph asked a rebel leader how he could forsake wine and songstresses in favor of fighting.

VI

The Prophetic charisma transcended man to places, which it endowed with the power to exercise magic over their receptive visitors. Medina was the City of the Prophet par excellence. Among its many honorific titles are Taybah (sweet, pleasant) and Munawwarah (the illumined, illustrious). It is formally styled today al-Madinah al-Munawwarah. Moslem geographers cite traditions to prove that it was favored with bountiful blessings. Its flowers are more fragrant and its fruits are more delicious than flowers and fruits elsewhere. A prayer in its Mosque is more efficacious than a prayer in a thousand mosques — exclusive, of course, of the Mecca one. In his chapter on Medina, ibn-al-Faqih of Hamadhan, whose geography written in 930 was a source for Yaqut and al-Maqdisi among others, cites a number of such traditions:

Plague shall not find its way into it, nor shall an Antichrist. In its perilous desert will the Antichrist perish. In it the Koran descended; the Divine ordinances were enjoined. In it the principles of religion and law and the regulations governing proper conduct and determining right and wrong were established. . . . All territories in the land of Islam have been acquired by the sword, except Medina; it was acquired by faith. Its soil, according to the Prophet, is a remedy for elephantiasis.[5]

In his long entry on Medina, Yaqut quotes certain traditions ascribed to the Prophet:

As Allah's Messenger (Allah's blessing and peace be upon him) was leaving Mecca to Medina, he said: "O Lord, Thou hast taken me out of a place dearest unto me, take me now to a place dearest unto Thee." Accordingly Allah made him settle in Medina. As he settled therein he said: "O Lord, grant us in it stability and ample sustenance." The Messenger then told his people: "He of you who can die in Medina, let him do so, and I shall be his witness and intercessor on the day of judgment." . . . He further said: "O Lord, Abraham, Thy slave, friend, prophet and messenger, beseeched Thee in behalf of the people of Mecca, so does Muhammad, Thy slave, prophet and messenger, beseech Thee now in behalf of the people of Medina for what Abraham had beseeched Thee: bless their measures and weights and bless their fruit."[6]

On his visit to Medina October 1326, ibn-Battutah made friends not only with sojourners in the city but also with the attendants in its Mosque, about one of whom he relates the following anecdote:

It is related that abu-'Abdullah al-Gharnati [from Spain] was a servant in the household of a shaykh named 'Abd-al-Hamid al-'Ajami [from Persia]. So much confidence did the shaykh have in his servant that he, when going on a trip, would trust him with his family and property. On a certain occasion he left him at home as usual and went away. The shaykh's wife fell in love with him and invited him to satisfy her, but he refused, saying, "Verily, I fear Allah and will not betray him who entrusted me with his family and property." But she insisted and pressed him to an extent that he feared to fall into the temptation. He therefore castrated himself and fell on the ground unconscious. There he remained until he was found. After treatment and recovery, he en-

5. Ibn-al-Faqih, *Kitab al-Buldan*, ed. M. J. de Goeje (Leyden, 1885), p. 23.

6. Yaqut, vol. IV, pp. 460, 461.

rolled in the service of the noble Mosque and became chief of the muezzins and attendants. He is still there alive.[7]

Of the European visitors to Mecca, several included Medina in their itineraries. Among them was the first in the series, Varthema.

In his brief account the Italian traveler compounded abuse with inaccuracy. Islam was a "sect of Mahomet"; abu-Bakr was a "cardinal who wanted to be pope." After three days in the city (Varthema arrived May 11, 1503), "being bored of these things and the vanities of Mahomet," he left with the caravan to Mecca. One point, however, should be brought out to Varthema's credit: he discredited the European myth relating to Muhammad's coffin. "Now, some who say that the body of Mahomet is suspended in the air at Mecca must be reproved. I have seen his sepulcher in this city Medinahalnabi [Medinat al-Nabi, the City of the Prophet], in which we remained three days, and wished to see everything."[8]

Badia, the learned Spaniard, missed Medina which was then (February 1807) in puritanical Wahhabi hands. En route from Jiddah his caravan was intercepted and he lost, among other things, his watch, but happily not his astronomical instruments. A collection of samples of insects, plants, and fossils he destroyed or threw away.

When Burckhardt entered Medina (January 27, 1814) it had passed to Egyptian rule under Ottoman suzerainty but still displayed the effects of the Wahhabi invasion. Of the three months he spent there two were marred by sickness of fever. In his *Travels* Burckhardt devotes almost an entire volume to Medina. The oval-shaped city is 2,800 paces in circuit surrounded by thick stone walls. Outside the walls are well-watered date plantations. Reportedly "upward of one hundred different sorts of dates grow in the immediate neighborhood." The interdiction against killing game and cutting trees in such a holy place is entirely ignored. Wheat and barley are the principal products of the fields. The houses are stone-built, flat-roofed, and two stories high. The streets are "often two or three paces across" and only the few important ones boast the luxury of stone pavement. Among these

7. Defrémery and Sanguinetti, Arabic text, vol. I, pp. 279–280; cf. Gibb, vol. I, p. 175.

8. The *Itinerary of Ludovico di Varthema of Bologna,* tr. John W. Winters, ed. R. C. Temple (London, 1928), p. 15.

is the main street from the Cairo gate to the Mosque. Most of the shops are on this street. There are only few merchants in town. Such is the dearth of mechanics that when repairs in the Mosque are required, mechanics are imported from Cairo or Constantinople. The population, 16,000 to 20,000 (including suburbs), is largely of foreign stock, replenished yearly by newcomers. The mortality is so high that otherwise the city could be depopulated. The most prevalent diseases are fevers. Dysenteries are rare. Medinese women are the only ones in the East who do not howl and cry on the death of a member of the family. The European stories about Muhammad's coffin are unknown.

Burckhardt's description of the Mosque's corner enclosing the Prophet's tomb reveals his powers of observation:

The gaudy colours displayed on every side, the glazed columns, fine carpets, rich pavement, the gilt inscriptions on the wall to the south, and the glittering railing of the Hedjrah [Hujrah, site of Muhammad's chamber] in the back-ground, dazzle the sight at first; but, after a short pause, it becomes evident that this is a display of tinsel decoration, and not of real riches. When we recollect that this spot is one of the holiest of the Mohammedan world, and celebrated for its splendour, magnificence, and costly ornaments, and that it is decorated with the united

Richard F. Burton, *Narrative of a Pilgrimage to al-Madinah and Mecca* (London, 1893), vol. i, p. 283

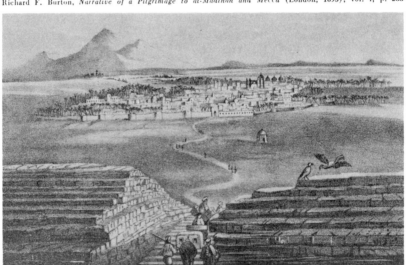

View of Medina, 1853

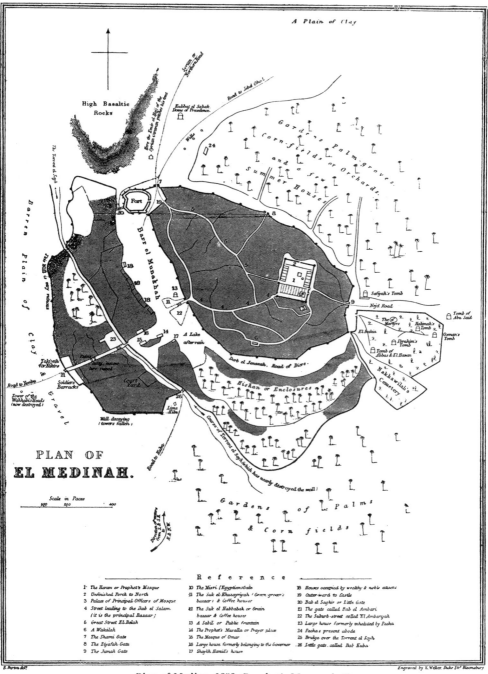

A Plain of Clay

High Basaltic Rocks

PLAN OF
EL MEDINAH.

Scale in Paces
100   200   400

Gardens of Palms
& Corn fields

R e f e r e n c e

1· The Haram or Prophet's Mosque
2 Unfinished Porch to North
3 Palace of Principal Officers of Mosque
4 Street leading to the Bab el Salam.
   (it is the principal Bazaar)
5 Great Street El Belah
6 A Wakilah
7 The Shami Gate
8 The Egyafah Gate
9 The Jumah Gate

10 The Misri (Egyptian Gate)
11 The Suk el Buzayriyah (Green grocers
    bazaar) & Coffee houses
12 The Suk el Habbabah or Grain
    bazaar & Coffee houses
13 A Sabil or Public fountain
14 The Prophet's Musalla or Prayer place
15 The Mosque of Omar
16 Large house formerly belonging to the Governor
17 Shaykh Hamid's house

18 Houses occupied by wealthy & noble citizens
19 Outer ward to Castle
20 Bab el Saghir or Little Gate
21 The gate called Bab el Ambari
22 The Suburb street called El Ambaryah
23 Large house formerly inhabited by Pacha
24 Pacha's present abode
25 Bridge over the Torrent el Sayh
26 Little gate called Bab Kuba

Plan of Medina, 1853 (Prophet's Mosque is 1)

59

pious donations of all the devotees of that religion, we are still more forcibly struck with its paltry appearance.[9]

To Richard Burton, who visited thirty-nine years after Burckhardt, the city seemed comfortable and flourishing. Houses, some of which were built of brick, featured latticed balconies. Of the 16,000 to 18,000 population, storekeepers were few. Manual labor was held in low esteem, being the monopoly of black slaves from Abyssinia. During his five-week sojourn the British visitor was hospitably entertained in the home of Shaykh Hamid.

Our life in Shaykh Hamid's house was quiet but not disagreeable. I never once set eyes upon the face of [a] woman, unless the African slave girls be allowed the title. Even these at first attempted to draw their ragged veils over their sable charms, and would not answer the simplest question; by degrees they allowed me to see them, and they ventured their voices to reply to me; still they never threw off a certain appearance of shame. I never saw, nor even heard, the youthful mistress of the household, who stayed all day in the upper rooms. The old lady, Hamid's mother, would stand upon the stairs, and converse aloud with her son, and, when few people were about the house, with me. . . .

To pass our *soirée*, we occasionally dressed in common clothes, shouldered a Nabbut [heavy stick], and went to the *café*; sometimes on festive occasions we indulged in a Taatumah (or Itmiyah), a late supper of sweetmeats, pomegranates, and dried fruits. Usually we sat upon mattresses spread upon the ground in the open air at the Shaykh's door; receiving evening visits, chatting, telling stories, and making merry, till each, as he felt the approach of the drowsy god, sank deep into his proper place, and fell asleep.[10]

Hostess to the expatriate Prophet, scene of his triumphs and place of his burial; home of his immediate successors and headquarters of the armies that destroyed one empire and humiliated another; home of the Companions and cradle of the Islamic tradition; a goal of the holy pilgrimage, al-Madinah al-Munawwarah holds second place after Mecca in the esteem and affections of believers the world over.

9. John L. Burckhardt, *Travels in Arabia*, vol. II (London, 1829), p. 177.

10. Richard F. Burton, *Personal Narrative of a Pilgrimage to Al-Madinah and Meccah*, ed. Isabel Burton, (London, 1893), vol. I, pp. 297–298, 300.

3

Damascus:

The Imperial Capital

If Paradise be on earth, Damascus must be it; if it is in heaven, Damascus can parallel and match it.

Ibn-Jubayr

Damascus is the gift of the Barada. The river gushes forth almost full grown immediately below Anti-Lebanon's watershed, rushes twenty-three miles down the slope, fans out into six main streams to irrigate a desert area and convert it into "one of the three earthly paradises." The sixteen by ten miles of gardens and orchards thus created, and named Ghutah, set the city like a pearl in an emerald girdle of green — a sight especially appreciated by peoples of barren lands. From the time of Naaman the Syrian general of the mid-ninth pre-Christian century, who raised the rhetorical question as to whether the waters of Damascus were not better than all those of Israel — including the Jordan (2 Kings 5:12) — to the present day, Damascenes have not ceased in poetry and prose to sing the beauty of their river and the fertility of their city. It is the favorite theme of their poets since Umayyad days. In fact, considering the length of service and the measure of usefulness, few cities have as much reason to be thankful to their rivers as Damascus has.

The Hebrews called the Barada (which in Arabic suggests the idea of ice-cold) Abana (stony). Classical writers had a more appropriate epithet for it, Chryshorrhoas (gold-pouring). The other Damascas river mentioned in 2 Kings 5:12, Pharpar, is now called al-A'waj. The A'waj, a confluence of several streams, rises in Mount Hermon, pursues a tortuous course (whence its Arabic name) and irrigates the plains south-east of the city.

But Damascus is more than an agricultural post. It is a desert port. Situated at the east end of a west-to-east trade route, it is itself a center of route radiation northward to its only rival in Syria — Aleppo — and thence to Asia Minor, southward to Palestine and on to Hijaz, and westward through an almost lifeless five hundred–mile desert to Baghdad, and through Baghdad to Mesopotamia and Persia. This makes of the oasis a trade and industry post. On the local scene Damascus provides a market of exchange for the Bedouins of the Syrian Desert.

Its people call it Dimashq, more fully Dimashq al-Sham (of Syria) and commonly simply al-Sham — as if the city were the entire country. A Damascene taxi driver in Beirut would not call out "'ala [to] Dimashq," but "'ala al-Sham." The term Dimashq does not admit of a Semitic etymology. It presumably goes back to a prehistoric non-Semitic origin. Recent excavations indicate an urban settlement of the fourth millennium B.C. on the site. In 1595 B.C. a Hittite monarch penetrated in Syria south to Damashunas, which sounds suspiciously like Damascus. But its first clear stepping on the threshold of written history comes a century and a half later when the Egyptian Thutmose III conducted several campaigns against Syria and listed Timasku or Damasku among the conquered towns. This gives it a life-span justifying its claim of being the longest continuously inhabited city known — a record of about 3,500 years with no known lapse to a village status.

I

Damascus made its debut on the royalty stage toward the end of the second millennium B.C. It then became the capital of an Aramaean kingdom that in its heyday extended from the Euphrates, through eastern Syria and Transjordan, to the Dead Sea. Originally Semitic nomads, the Aramaeans first settled in Mesopotamia, then penetrated into Syria, where they assimilated the cultures of their Amorite and Phoenician cousins. The Lebanons intercepted their expansion westward. One of the early groups that later coalesced to form the Hebrew nation in Palestine belonged to this Aramaean migration. Hebrew tradition kept a vague memory of that fact. In one place (Deut. 26:5) it calls Abraham — the father of the nation — Aramaean ("Syrian" in the Authorized Version; cf. 2 Sam. 8:5; 1 Kings 15:18). In another place (Gen. 24:4; 29:21 seq.) it makes the maternal ancestry of Jacob's children Aramaeans. Besides equating Aram with Syria, the Old Testament uses the term both individually and collectively (Gen. 10:22,23; 1 Chron. 1:17).

Aramaean Damascus rose to power contemporaneously with the Hebrew Kingdom and contiguously to it. The two soon became foes involved in intermittent warfare. This, unfortunately for both, synchronized with the rise of a more formidable power to the north, Assyria. The Assyrian empire sought westward expansion for control of the trade routes and for reaching the Mediterranean ports. With one hand Damascus had to ward off Assyrian aggression, and with the other Hebrew advances. King David reached and for a time occupied and garrisoned Damascus (2 Sam. 8:5; 1 Chron. 18:5–6), but the division of his monarchy in 922 worked to the Aramaean advantage.

Under Ben-Hadad I (ca. 870–843) and his successor, Damascus reached the limit of its potential. Naaman was one of Ben-Hadad's generals. He was a leper but leprosy in Syria carried no stigma as it did in Israel. The Kingdom of Israel became nominally a Damascus vassal and when King Ahab either refused to pay the tribute or to cooperate against the threatening Assyrian attack, Ben-Hadad moved to coerce him and reached his capital, Samaria. At the battle of Qarqar on the Orontes in 853, the Syrian coalition of 60,000 men — to which Phoenician city-states as well as Israel contributed contingents — confronted the Assyrian Shalmaneser III and his troops. The contest ended in a draw. Damascus' share comprised 1,200 chariots, 1,200 horses, and 20,000 infantry.

Ben-Hadad's successor Hazael (d. ca. 805) pushed his conquests southward not only at the expense of Israel but of Judah. He reached the Arnon (2 Kings 10:32–33), today al-Mujib, which empties into the Dead Sea north of Karak. He then "set his face to go up to Jerusalem," capital of Judah, but was bought off by the gold and treasures of the royal palace and the Temple (2 Kings 12:17–18).

But battling against Israel-Judah was one thing and bucking the Assyrian military machine was another. In 733 Tiglath-pileser III moved against Damascus (Dimashqa in cuneiform inscriptions). King Rezin, after a battle, took to flight and, in the words of the Assyrian bulletin, "like a mouse he entered the gate of his city," where he was finally (732) slain (2 Kings 6:9). The city's inhabitants were deported (cf. Is. 17:1), the trees of its orchards — its pride through the ages — were cut down, "not one escaped." Its sixteen provinces with their 591 cities were, again to borrow the words of the Assyrian invader, destroyed "like mounds left by a flood." Assyria was determined that no more should a power challenge her right to supremacy in the Fertile Crescent.

The Aramaean kingdom of Damascus passed away, but the Aramaean heritage passed on. In the course of the two centuries of Damascus' ascendancy, Aramaean merchants came near monopolizing the hinterland trade as their Phoenician rivals had monopolized the maritime trade. What turned out to be its most enduring export, however, was language. By 500 b.c. Aramaic had established itself as the language of commerce, culture, and government from the Mediterranean to the Tigris. More than that it replaced the vernaculars. Christ's mother tongue was Aramaic. Hebrew was reserved for synagogue and school use. In its Syriac dialect, Aramaic still figures in the liturgies of Eastern Churches, including the Maronite of Lebanon. Jews carried Aramaic with them to Arabia, Egypt, Persia, and other lands of the Diaspora. Darius I (522–486) made it the interprovincial language of his empire. Aramaic remained the lingua franca of the entire area until the conquest of Alexander the Great.

With the spread of language went the alphabet. Borrowed from their Phoenician neighbors, this ingenious system of writing was transmitted by Aramaeans to the Hebrews, the Arabians, the Persians, the Hindus, and other peoples of the East. Along with the linguistic went the religious heritage. Hadad, the storm god heading the Aramaean pantheon, was metamorphosed by the Romans into Jupiter Damascenus and his worship was carried into Rome. His consort Atargatis, the "Syrian goddess" of the Greeks and Romans, was often confused with the Phoenician Astarte, goddess of fertility and love, and in places identified with the correspondent Greek Aphrodite. The Romans built a temple for Atargatis in their capital.

The conquest of Syria in 333 b.c. by Alexander the Great marked the opening of a new era for the entire region — an era of Greco-Roman dominion and cultural infiltration that was not to end until the rise of Islam a thousand years later. The past capital of Aram and future capital of Islam sank into relative oblivion and there remained throughout the entire period.

By way of implementing the conqueror's policy of Hellenizing the conquered territory, Alexander's general and successor Seleucus I Nicator built in 300 B.C. — among other cities — one on the Orontes named after his son Antiochus. Not only did Antioch become the seat of the Western Seleucid Kingdom but a leading center of trade and industry. On the occupation of Syria by the Romans in 64 B.C., Damascus was bypassed in favor of Antioch as capital of the province of Syria. The Seleucid capital was more accessible from the sea and less oriented toward the desert. Antioch rose to a third place in the East after Constantinople and Alexandria.

In Roman times not only Antioch but other neighbors of Damascus eclipsed it. Throughout, scarce notice was given the defunct capital by classical writers, who took full note of Beirut (Berytus) and its famous school of law and of Baalbak (Ba'labakk, Heliopolis), the "city of the sun" and the site of the majestic temple of Jupiter Optimus Maximus Heliopolitanus. Roman rule over Damascus was briefly interrupted by the North Arabian Nabataeans, based in Petra, who held the city at the time of Paul's conversion. The "street called Straight" (Acts 9:11) bears today the name of Midhat Pasha, a nineteenth-century Ottoman governor, and the place on the city wall near the east gate from which the apostle took to flight is still pointed out to curious tourists. In 395, when the Eastern Roman Empire (Byzantine) achieved its final separation from the West, Damascus was made capital of a minor district embracing Hims (Emesa), Baalbak, and Tadmur (Palmyra). For its full rejuvenation it had to wait until the rise of Islam.

II

Mu'awiyah's choice of Damascus in 661 as the capital of his caliphate was perhaps the most pregnant fact in its entire history. It started the city on its way to becoming, for eighty-nine years (661–750), mistress of the Moslem realm and key city in world affairs. Its distance from the sea and its location in the shadow of a double-mountain wall were — in the absence of an Arab fleet — an advantage. The mountain did, however, shut off the cooling vapor-laden westerlies, leaving the city an average of 10 inches of rain and giving it a summer heat exceeding 100°F.; but the mountain compensated by originating Barada and al-A'waj and reducing humidity.

The high-water marks in the period of Damascus' Arab ascendancy may be summarized under three main headings: Mu'awiyah's achievements, the period of glory, and the decline and fall.

Mu'awiyah's name became as inextricably associated with Damascus as Muhammad's with Mecca and 'Umar's with Medina. He was the father of its dynasty — the Umayyad; the founder of its tradition; and the architect of its imperial institutions. Mu'awiyah the caliph built on his experience as governor, and his experience had the Byzantine model to follow. Under him Islam began to breathe more of the Mediterranean and less of the desert.

The Damascus caliph's starting point was, predictably, the military. Hitherto, the unit in warfare as in peace was the tribe, each under its own shaykh. Soon after the occupation of Syria, Mu'awiyah realized the archaic character of the system and started updating it in the manner of the Byzantine army. The new units consisted of trained, disciplined men, of varied tribes, receiving higher and more regular pay and accepting orders from professional officers. He meanwhile realized that his position in the land was untenable so long as he lacked naval protection against the greatest sea power in the eastern Mediterranean. For a start he did not have far to go. In Acre ('Akka) and Tyre (Sur), the Byzantines had left fully equipped shipyards (*dar al-sina'ah*, whence Eng. arsenal), with trained craftsmen and experienced sailors. The cedars of Lebanon were still there to offer their superb wood.

As early as 649, the new Arab admiral (from Ar. *amir al-bahr*, commander of the sea) was in a position to undertake his first naval expedition and occupy Cyprus. Caliph 'Umar unenthusiastically endorsed the expedition. He did not want the sea to intervene between him and his generals, nor did he want them to go where he could not reach them on a camel. Six years later the Moslem fleet had its first major encounter with the Christian — commanded by Emperor Constans II — on the Lycian coast in Asia Minor and almost destroyed it. By tying their ships to the enemies', the Arabs converted the sea fight into a land fight. The disaster thus inflicted on Constans was no less than that that had befallen his grandfather Heraclius at the Yarmuk.

With the military, the financial had first priority. Here more than merely following the Byzantine pattern, the Moslem ruler kept the Syrian Christian members of the family of St. John, whose father had in 635 secretly opened the city gates to the Arabian besiegers, in charge of the treasury. Greek was maintained as the language of the books. In the eastern half of the empire, Persian was not disturbed. What else could a new ruler — lacking the personnel and the tradition — do? For administrative purposes the old provincial divisions in both the Byzantine and the Persian realms were, with some modifications, maintained. The different provinces of the empire were linked with a postal service system relayed on horses. Primarily intended to serve governmental interests, the system added espionage to its function, making every postmaster a member of the intelligence service. The pre-Arabian currency throughout the caliphate was kept with no change. Some time had to pass before Arab coinage was struck.

For years the Damascus court was to an extent dominated by Christians. Mu'awiyah included in his harem a daughter of a South Arabian Christianized tribe domiciled in the Syrian Desert. It was her son Yazid whom he, in the interest of stability and continuity and in defiance of caliphal tradition, designated as his successor. In the Orthodox regime of Medina the caliphal form of election had for background the tribal system according to which the elders elected a qualified senior member to the shaykhdom.

Mu'awiyah's poet laureate, al-Akhtal, was likewise a Christian. Al-Akhtal would enter the caliphal palace with the cross dangling from his neck. As an Arabian, Mu'awiyah had full appreciation of the role playable by the poet as a publicity agent and as a molder of public opinion. Almost all the caliph's subjects in the Fertile Crescent and in Egypt were, it should be recalled, still Christians. The religious barrier in those days did not loom high, and the caliph's tolerant policy made it look lower. Chroniclers report debates in the caliphal court on the relative merits of the two religions. Among the writings of St. John (d. 740) were two dialogues between a Christian and a "Saracen" intended as a manual for Christians' guidance in their arguments with Moslems. For his tolerance Mu'awiyah was repaid in undivided loyalty by his Christian subjects.

The caliph displayed no less ability in handling tribal affairs. He pitted one tribe against another and deftly played one party against another. Against North Arabians, with whom he was not a favorite, he cultivated South Arabians. Certain shaykhs he bribed; others he persuaded. When the 'Alids, in whose eyes he was an outright usurper, set up against him 'Ali's eldest son al-Hasan, Mu'awiyah immediately secured from the claimant — by what we call today a blank check on the treasury — a definite renunciation of all claims. This was indeed a masterstroke. The following words attributed to him sum up his philosophy of rule: "I apply not my lash where my tongue suffices, nor my sword where my whip is enough. And if there be one hair binding me to my fellow men I let it not break. If they pull I loosen, and if they loosen I pull."[1] The honorific title of "one of the four Arab geniuses" bestowed on him by posterity was indeed well deserved.

With the realm relatively pacified though not consolidated, the Damascus caliph felt in a position to renew the holy war interrupted by the civil disturbances. Therewith the second wave of conquest began. The eastern sector Mu'awiyah entrusted to his lieutenants. There they pushed the frontier across the Oxus to Bukhara and Samarqand and south of the river to Kabul (in what is now Afghanistan). The newly acquired cities became brilliant centers of Islamic culture and learning as well as bulwarks of militant Islam. An initial contact was thereby established with a new racial element, the Turkish, different from the Indo-European and Semitic and related to the Mongolian. When the Arab creators and protagonists of Islam became anemic and degenerate, it was new Turkish converts who championed its cause and perpetuated its mission. They built its greatest and most enduring empire in modern times.

The caliph concerned himself primarily with the West, where enemy number one lurked. His aim was no less than the capture of Constantinople, haughty headquarters of Greek Orthodoxy and an impregnable land and sea base. After a number of recurring raids into the "land of the Romans" (Asia Minor), intended for booty and keeping militarily fit rather than for occupancy, the Syrian army at last reached Chalcedon, the Asian suburb of the capital. The year was 668; Muhammad had been dead for only thirty-six years and the army included in its personnel his host at Medina. For the first time Arab

1. Al-Yaʿqubi, *Taʾrikh,* ed. M. Th. Houtsma (Leyden, 1883), vol. ii, p. 283.

eyes gazed covetously at the splendors of the city across the Bosporus. The prospects looked bright and the caliph's son Yazid was rushed with fresh recruits. The siege was pressed against a city protected by a triple wall, high towers, and powerful fortifications. Besides, the invaders had no protection against cold, smallpox, and privations.

Damascus was disappointed but not disheartened. In 674 another attempt was made, this time a naval one. The fleet succeeded in establishing a base on a peninsular projection from Asia to the southern bank of the Sea of Marmara. For seven years the invaders harassed the city, encountering this time a new enemy, the so-called Greek fire. This was a secret weapon consisting of a highly combustible compound that burned even on or under water. The early champions of Islam had to yield the highly coveted prize to late recruits, the Turks, and wait almost eight centuries to see the crescent and star replace the cross over Santa Sophia.

Byzantine North Africa was entrusted by Mu'awiyah to his lieutenant 'Uqbah ibn-Nafi', a nephew of 'Amr ibn-al-'As. 'Uqbah began where his maternal uncle had ended. By 670 he had penetrated into Tunisia, where he built, with material from the ruins of Carthage, Qayrawan (Kairouan). Originally intended, as the term implies, to be a depot of arms, the new city became the capital of Moslem Africa; its mosque took its place after those of Mecca, Medina, Jerusalem, and Damascus as the holiest place. 'Uqbah pushed on to Biskra in Algeria, where his tomb has developed into a holy shrine frequented by pilgrims revering in Sidi (my lord) 'Uqbah a father of Moslem Africa. Being on the same general cultural level as the Arabians, the Berbers found the new masters more congenial than the old ones. In a few generations they were more Islamized and Arabicized than they had been Romanized or Hellenized in centuries.

Aside from political enemies Mu'awiyah had critics and detractors from among theologians and historians, mostly 'Alids and 'Abbasids. The genuineness of his conversion was questioned and suspected as having been one of convenience rather than conviction. The legitimacy of his caliphate was denied. The "innovations" in his regime included secularization of the caliphate, changing it into a monarchy, erecting a throne in his palace for himself as king (*malik*, a detestable term then), surrounding himself with a bodyguard and setting in the mosque a box in which to sit during the service. In violation of the traditional caliphal succession, he nominated his son, a winebibber, women-chaser, music and sport lover, to succeed him. The fact, however, remains that after Muhammad and 'Umar, Mu'awiyah stands out as one of the ablest men in the history of the Arabs.

III

The glory that was Damascus covered the regimes of the fifth caliph 'Abd-al-Malik (685–705) and his son al-Walid (705–715). This was the time in which the definite subjugation of Transoxiana was accomplished, the reconquest and pacification of North Africa achieved, and the conquest of Spain undertaken. It was also the time in which the Arabicization of the state administration was effected and the earliest monumental structures erected. Never before and never after did the Syrian capital reach such a peak of power and glory.

'Abd-al-Malik started his career under unpromising conditions. Three pretenders contested his right to the throne: an 'Alid, a Khariji, and, more formidably, a Medinese, 'Abdullah ibn-al-Zubayr. Ibn-al-Zubayr was then recognized by Hijaz, South Arabia, and Iraq. He and the 'Alid contender al-Husayn, second son of 'Ali, had cherished their ambitions for long, but dared not commit an overt act till Mu'awiyah's death. In fact 'Abd-al-Malik found himself facing a second civil war.

On the battlefield of Karbala', northwest of Kufah, a general of Yazid on October 10, 680, slew the Prophet's grandson, sent his head to Damascus, and bequeathed his followers a martyr and a passion day which they have not ceased to commemorate to the present. But 'Abdullah ibn-al-Zubayr, a maternal cousin of the Prophet and a nephew of his wife 'A'ishah, was left to 'Abd-al-Malik's general al-Hajjaj ibn-Yusuf to deal with. The pretender sought asylum, as he had done once before, in the Meccan Haram, but again the sanctity of the place was violated. There he was slaughtered in 692. 'Abd-al-Malik's victory over ibn-al-Zubayr is comparable to that of Mu'awiyah over 'Ali. In both cases Islam was to an extent torn from its habitat with its tribal and nomadic background, established in a new environment, and offered new and wider horizons. Damascus met the challenge of the two holier cities and pursued its course.

Having restored Hijaz to the Umayyad fold, al-Hajjaj proceeded to do likewise with the rest of Arabia and with Iraq, a hot bed of Shi'ism. The former schoolteacher of Ta'if became in Iraq the mailed fist of the Umayyad caliphate. No measure was too ruthless for him to take against secessionists and deviationists, no head too high to reach, no neck too stiff to wring. His victims were counted by the thousands, hundreds of thousands in Shi'ite sources. The second civil war therewith came to an end. Iraq was pacified. The stage was set for a third wave of conquest, following those of 'Umar and Mu'awiyah.

It was al-Hajjaj as viceroy and his lieutenants and successors who brought about the final reduction of what had been in the east overrun in Mu'awiyah's time. It was in reality a reconquest followed by expansion through Turkestan, Baluchistan, and Punjab. From Kufah and Basrah the campaigns were conducted through Persia with the aid of Persian recruits. It was a double thrust: one moving eastward through Turkestan and the other southward through the northwestern region of India. It continued during all al-Walid's reign. In 711 Daybul at the mouth of the Indus was captured, after two earlier attempts by sea, and the city developed into an illustrious center of Islam. Two years later Multan, north on an affluent of the Indus in Punjab, followed suit, and for almost three centuries functioned as Arab capital of the region and Moslem outpost. Farther northeast Kashghar, capital city of eastern Turkestan near the Chinese border, was captured (715). Kashghar marks the farthest limit ever reached.

The acquisition of Turkestan gave Islam the religion a permanent lodging in central Asia, and Islam the state the control of the so-called silk route, an international highway linking the Far to the Near East and sending ramifications north and south. India, into which Islam expanded later, offered the conquerors contact with a developed religion, Buddhism, and access to fabulous mineral resources and warm hospitality for their faith. Today Islam claims the allegiance of about 57,000,000 in India proper, and in Pakistan, independent since 1956, about 96,000,000. From Turkestan and Hindustan — to use India's Arabic name — the new religion penetrated by peaceful methods to Indonesia, which today claims about 100,000,000 Moslems, comparable to the number of all Arab Moslems.

The last decade of the seventh century marked the attainment of maturity by the Moslem state. It was time to nationalize its institutions and Arabicize its administration. The step was conditioned by the availability of Arab manpower, and necessitated by the pressing need for increasing the common denominator for a heterogeneous society. Accordingly Christian officials in the chancellery, exchequer, and courts were replaced by Arabic-speaking, Arabic-writing officials. In Persia, then ruled from Basrah and Kufah, Persian was replaced likewise by Arabic. In Egypt Arabic again was substituted for the native language, Coptic. With the linguistic change went change in currency. The earliest Arab coins display koranic superscriptions stamped on Byzantine and Sasanid coins and at times, in imitation of the current coinage, show the figure of a standing caliph. 'Abd-al-Malik was the first to strike purely Arab dirhams and dinars. He fixed on the severe nonpictorial epigraphic type. In 696 this caliph struck in Damascus the first gold dinars using no iconography whatever. The epigraphic type then introduced became characteristic of Moslem coinage to the present day. Meantime government bureaus were multiplied and their facilities expanded. The bureau of postal service was the recipient of special attention. A reform of a different character attributed to al-Hajjaj related to the 'Uthmanic text of the Koran, then written in consonants only. Vowel signs were added to facilitate reading and avoid ambiguity.

But 'Abd-al-Malik's most conspicuous monument lay in another field, that of building. When the two Holy Cities of Hijaz were still in an anti-caliph's hands, the caliph commenced building a mosque that would divert pilgrimage to Jerusalem, outshine its Holy Sepulcher, and provide believers with a place of worship worthy of their new position as masters of a world. Result: The Dome of the Rock, a gem of architecture still unsurpassed in grandeur and majesty anywhere in Arab lands. The rock on which it rose was the traditional halting place of the Prophet's mount on his nocturnal ascent heavenward (sur. 17:1). The Dome is in reality the shrine of an adjacent mosque also built by 'Abd-al-Malik (perhaps completed by his son) and named later al-Masjid al-Aqsa (the farther mosque, cited in the above quoted verse). The entire area is one of the most hallowed on the surface of the earth, having once been the site of the Jewish Temple, a Roman place of worship, and a Christian church. The Aqsa has ever remained a living symbol of the religion of Muhammad. The wave of indignation that

The Dome of the Rock, Jerusalem

swept across the world of Islam when, in the summer of 1969, an Australian religious fanatic, set the structure on fire, testifies to that fact.

By 'Abd-al-Malik's time social classes had become well marked. The

73

ladder was topped, of course, by the caliphal family. Arabian Moslems came next, forming a hereditary aristocracy. They lived largely in cities, functioned as governors, army officers, court officials, and large landowners. They occupied quarters of their own according to tribal affiliation. Then came Neo-Moslems. These were Syrians, Persians, and other conquered nationals adopting Islam and, theoretically, standing on a par with early professors of the faith. Below them came Dhimmis, mainly Christians and Jews, professors of revealed religions. They continued in the practice of their occupations — commercial, mechanical, agricultural — and, till the post-Umayyad period, constituted the bulk of the population. At the bottom of the ladder stood the slaves, recruited by purchase and from unransomed prisoners of war. A Moslem could not enslave a coreligionist but was not under obligation to enfranchise him if while in slavery he professed Islam.

The Damascene street scene must have presented an early version of what it is today. In the narrow, covered streets, with no right or left rule of way, all members of society — Greeks, Aramaeans, Bedouins, Arabians, speaking different tongues, wearing diverse styles of clothes — freely rubbed shoulders. Sherbet peddlers and pastry vendors raised their voices in competition with the tramp of pedestrians, donkeys, and camels. Just as noise filled the ears, so did smell fill the nose and color satisfy the eyes. Veiled women briskly crossed the streets; they could make up for what they missed by peering through the latticed windows of their houses. Occasionally an aristocrat dressed in aba, riding a horse and accompanied by his slaves would make an appearance and the passers-by would make way.

Al-Walid continued in the building tradition of his father. He renovated the Haram of Medina, enlarged and beautified that of Mecca, and erected schools, hospitals, and other public buildings in Damascus. In the first year of his reign (705) he began in his capital the erection of a mosque now called Umayyad Mosque. Considered the fourth sacred sanctuary after those of Mecca, Medina, and Jerusalem this mosque is the most enduring monument of this caliph. His predecessors in Damascus were satisfied with worship in an unpretentious palace built by Mu'awiyah near his residence al-Khadra' (the green building), a remodeled Byzantine governor's palace. Al-Walid was not. He began by confiscating the basilica of St. John the Baptist, adjoin-

Inside the Umayyad Mosque. The domed structure is said to hold the head of John the Baptist. The pulpit is to the right in the background

ing the old mosque and standing on the site of a Roman temple dedicated to Jupiter Damascenus, originally a temple of the Syrian Hadad. The "burial place" of St. John's head is still shown under a gilded dome inside the building. The minarets of the new mosque, the first of their kind, were modeled after the church tower and in turn served as a model for muezzins' towers from Syria to Spain. The caliph reportedly employed Syrian and Byzantine architects together with Persian and Indian craftsmen, expending the annual land revenue of Syria as well as eighteen shiploads of gold and silver from Cyprus. Local talent was supplemented by imported specialists from Constantinople requested from the emperor. Artists adorned the building, among other things, with mural representations of cities and trees in gold and precious stones, which hid behind a plaster cover imposed by some pious ruler until rediscovered in 1928. The Palestinian geographer al-Maqdisi visited the city about 985, when it was ruled from Egypt, and left us a vivid description of the decoration:

The walls of the mosque, to a height of two men, are faced with multi-colored marble, and from there to the ceiling with mosaics bearing representations of trees and towns and displaying inscriptions, all the ultimate in beauty, elegance and artistry. Hardly a known tree or town does not figure on the walls. The column capitals are covered with gold; portico arches are ornamented with mosaics. . . . The mihrab[2] and its surroundings are covered with carnelian and turquoise stones of the largest possible size. To the left of it is another mihrab, reserved for the use of the sultan who, at a cost — I was told — of 500 dinars, renovated it.[3]

In the military field, al-Walid's reign has as much to take pride in as in the building field. For it was then that Islam conquered and held the first European country. In North Africa as in central Asia, so loose was the first Umayyad hold on the conquered territory that it had to be reconquered before it could be pacified, integrated, and used as a stepping-stone for further conquests. That was what 'Uqbah's two successors, under 'Abd-al-Malik and his successor, undertook. They pushed the frontier to the Atlantic, opening the way to the invasion of Europe. From his capital in Qayrawan, Viceroy Musa ibn-Nusayr ordered his Berber freedman Tariq to proceed. In the tradition of earlier caliphs, al-Walid objected to a full-scale campaign. On July 19, 711, Tariq, with 12,000 men, mostly Berbers, landed at the foot of the mighty rock to be known thereafter as Gibraltar, a corruption of Jabal (mount of) Tariq. Near the mouth of the Barbate (now Salado) River he faced on July 19, 711, an army of 25,000 under its Visigothic king Roderick. It was a decisive encounter. The king disappeared, probably drowned in the river and then carried away into the sea. The march through the southern half of the Peninsula was more of a promenade than a military one. In a little more than a year Toledo, the capital, betrayed by Jewish citizens, was entered. The entire Visigothic Kingdom must have been rotten at the core. Spaniards considered Visigothic rule alien and oppressive and felt exploited by overlords and bishops. Of all astounding victories of Arabs this one, considering the distance from its base and its conduct by non-Arabs, is perhaps the most astounding in its achievement and results.

2. Niche in the wall marking the kiblah.

3. Al-Maqdisi, *Ahsan al-Taqasim fi Ma'rifat al-Aqalim*, ed. M. J. de Goeje (Leyden, 1877), pp. 157–158. For a full translation see Guy Le Strange in *Palestine Pilgrims' Text Society*, vol. III (London, 1895), pp. 17 seq.

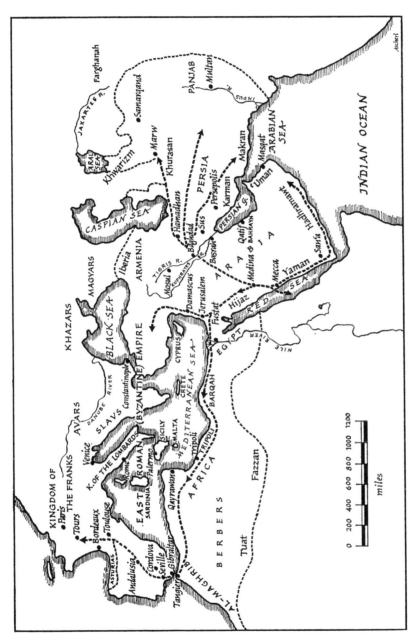

Arab Empire at its height, ca. 750

DAMASCUS

Jealous, Musa followed with 10,000 Syrian and Arabian troops. He wanted a share in the booty and honor and had to no effect ordered his freedman to halt. The victorious march was resumed. After whipping his lieutenant for insubordination, Musa was himself ordered back to Damascus to answer similar charges by his chief. The viceroy had acted independently on more than one occasion. He had even minted coins in his name.

At the head of a stately train of Visigothic princes and a retinue of slaves and mounts loaded with treasures of booty, Musa made his way through North Africa and southern Syria. He was received in February 715 with dignity and decorum in the courtyard of the newly built mosque close by the caliphal palace. The day, one of the proudest in Arab annals, was a day of disgrace for the conqueror of North Africa and Spain. Stripped of all power and property, Musa was last seen begging for food in a remote village of Hijaz. Under al-Walid's successors the Pyrenees were crossed, and raids into France reached in 732 the neighborhood of Tours. In no other time, ancient or medieval, did a realm assume such dimensions — from the Chinese border to the Atlantic.

IV

The pole on which Damascus climbed to the summit turned out to be a slippery one. Between the zenith and the nadir (both terms of Arabic etymology) there was room for no more than one generation. Of the eight caliphs in the period (715–750) two only were worthy of the heritage generated by Mu'awiyah and enriched by 'Abd-al-Malik and al-Walid. The remaining six, three of whom were sons of slave mothers, were incompetent, some dissolute if not degenerate. The brother-successor of al-Walid was more interested in drinking, hunting, and listening to song and music than in conducting state affairs. His son excelled the father. He spent more time in his pleasure houses in the desert, where their ruins are still visible, than in the capital. He is said to have indulged himself in swimming in a pool of wine and gulping enough of it to lower its surface. More than an incorrigible libertine, this caliph once committed an act of unusual sacrilege: making a target of a Koran copy for the arrows of his bow. Clearly, the sudden increase of wealth, the superabundance of slaves and concubines, the multiplied facilities for indulgence in luxury, and other characteristic vices of an affluent urban civilization — against which sons of the desert had developed no measure of immunity — were beginning to sap Arab vitality.

Other elements of weakness were inherent in the structure of the caliphal system, based on the assumption that the realm could be held together under the Arab scepter with religion serving as the binding force. The Arabic language then had no such words as state or citizen. The first to join the emerging state were Bedouins, who could not, even if they wanted, outlive their tribalism, particularism, and parochial loyalty. Moslem North Arabians and South Arabians were not slow to discover that the centuries-old ethnic-cultural gap was not exactly filled. As the empire expanded it multiplied its problems. By an irony of which history seems to be fond, the greater the success the empire achieved the deeper it dug its grave. The more Persians, Turks, Hindus, Berbers, and Spaniards were added, the more disproportionate the numbers of Arabs and non-Arabs became, and the weaker the structure became.

More specific factors came at last into play. Decline in the central authority made potential foes activists. Shi'ites, who had never acquiesced in the established order and considered all Umayyads impious usurpers, came out with their candidate, a descendant of 'Ali. Pietists, shocked by the worldliness of Umayyad caliphs, charged them all with deviation from puritanical Islam. Socially and economically discontented, the Neo-Moslems — particularly Persians and Iraqis — were ready to join any rebellious leader. Thus all necessary ingredients were there, with only one lacking: a catalyst.

The catalyst before long appeared in the person of abu-al-'Abbas, a descendant of al-'Abbas, Muhammad's uncle. Abu-al-'Abbas had good credentials, descending from a clan closer of kin to the Prophet and earlier in conversion to Islam. The new claimant made Iraq his headquarters and had his agent start the uprising in Persia. In October 749 public homage was paid him as caliph in the Kufah mosque. Three months later his troops met a Syrian army at the Great Zab, an affluent of the Tigris, and dealt it a crushing blow. The commander in chief Marwan (744–750) entered the battle as the fourteenth Umayyad caliph; he left it as the last of the line. He fled to Egypt, was caught hiding in a church, and decapitated. His head was sent to the victor. His capital surrendered after a brief siege.

In sharp contrast to the treatment accorded the family of his predecessor, abu-al-'Abbas embarked on a policy of extermination against the fallen house. His generals pursued its members throughout the land. Finally they resorted to a ruse. An invitation to a banquet outside of Jaffa (Yafa) was extended and eighty princes, considering it a gesture of conciliation, responded. But no sooner had they begun to eat than the hosts fell upon the guests and butchered them one by one. They then spread leather covers on the corpses and proceeded with the meal. Not only were the living to be punished but the dead, too. Caliphal tombs in Damascus were desecrated and their contents exhumed. Abu-al-'Abbas was styled al-Saffah (bloodshedder), a title he fully deserved.

Only one prince escaped the general massacre, a nineteen-year-old descendant of the tenth caliph. It was this 'Abd-al-Rahman who dramatically escaped from his 'Abbasid pursuers and, in disguise, trudged across Palestine, Egypt, and North Africa, landing five years later (755) in Spain. There single-handedly the refugee succeeded, after trials and tribulations, in establishing himself at Cordova as the master of the Peninsula and the founder of a new dynasty. Dead in Damascus, the Umayyad dynasty was born in Cordova.

V

The blackout that enveloped Damascus was total and prolonged. The torch passed on to Baghdad, where it shone brilliantly at times and flickered faintly at others, but never penetrating the Syrian border. Damascus' two predecessors, Mecca and Medina, inherited Prophetic charisma and an annual pilgrimage to sustain them indefinitely. The Syrian capital inherited neither grace.

As the 'Abbasid empire began to disintegrate, splinter states arose at its expense but none chose the defunct capital as a seat. For long centuries Damascus was ruled from Egypt by states nominally dependent on Baghdad and then entirely independent. This of course, did not preclude Damascus' serving as a provincial seat of government. Even when the Syrian Hamdanid state arose, Damascus was bypassed. The founder of the state, Sayf-al-Dawlah (944–967), chose Aleppo

Modern Damascus intersected by the Parliament Boulevard
with the Ghutah in the background

(Halab) for capital. Sayf renewed the war against the Byzantines and
made of Aleppo a military as well as a literary center. His court attracted some of the most illustrious scholars and littérateurs of the age,
such as the philosopher and musician al-Farabi and the renowned poet
al-Mutanabbi.

Only once did Damascus come near seizing the opportunity to restore some of its past glory. In 1154 Nur-al-Din, originally a Turk from
Mosul and already a master of Aleppo, wrested Damascus from the
hands of other Turks (Saljuqs) and made it his seat for attack on the
Crusaders' kingdom of Jerusalem. For the first time since Umayyad
days, Damascus began to function as a capital, albeit of a tiny state.
The city entered upon a brief period of renaissance. Nur enriched it
with new buildings, religious and educational, that are still among its
showplaces. One building he started houses today the prestigious Arab

Academy. On Nur's death in 1174, his former vassal and now hero of the anti-Crusades, Salah-al-Din (Saladin), occupied Damascus and made it a joint capital with Cairo of his Syro-Egyptian realm. The partition of the kingdom on Salah-al-Din's death (1193) among his brothers, sons and nephews extinguished all hope Damascus might have cherished of recapturing its past position.

In 1250 the Mamluks fell heirs to the dynasty founded by Salah-al-Din and in 1517 passed it on to the Ottoman Turks. Toward the end of that century when international trade began to assume new dimensions, Aleppo beat Damascus to becoming the new commercial center of the area. By the seventeenth century Venetians, French, English, and Dutch had established in it consulates and trade offices. Imports from Europe, such as cloth, metals, chemicals, and glass, arrived via Alexandria or Tripoli (Lebanon) to be exported from Aleppo to Asia Minor, Kurdistan, and Persia. In the meantime the English East India Company had virtually monopolized the spice trade of India, besides tapping the silk resources of China, and was making full use of the Aleppine market on its land trade route. At the termination of the French mandate in 1943 Damascus for the first time in twelve hundred years had its first full chance of becoming the capital of an independent state. The republican was the form chosen for the government.

VI

Moslem traditions revered in Damascus a birthplace of Abraham (grandfather of the Arabian nation), a goal of a visit by Muhammad, a refuge for Mary and her Son, and a subject of a koranic reference. Abraham, so the story goes, was born in Damascus or in a place outside of it to the north where his name is borne by a mosque (Masjid Ibrahim). Contact between Abraham and Damascus had pre-Islamic origin in the Old Testament (Gen. 14:15; 15:2). When still in his early teens — the legend continues — Muhammad joined a Mecca-Damascus caravan and after days' travel in the desert, his eyes fell on the orchard-ringed multicolored city and he hesitated to enter it for he wanted to enter Paradise but once. When unmarried Mary delivered her baby and sought a hiding place, the angel referred her to an "elevated spot, secure and abundant in water" (sur. 23:52). That spot must be, commentators say, Damascus, lying at the foot of Mt. Qasiyun, a projection of the Anti-Lebanon, and rising to a height of 2,400 feet above the sea. Commentators further claim that "Iram with the pillars" in the Koran (89:6) is likewise Damascus. Other than the phonetic relation between "Iram" and "Aram" no reason is evident.

These and other traditions have been reiterated through the ages by Arab geographers. Poets and writers since early Arab days never tire of singing the splendors of this beauty spot. The title of Fayha' (diffusive) given it has the idea of fragrance implied. All agree that the city is an earthly Paradise. Following are two specimens:

Said al-Asma'i,[4] "The paradises on earth are three: The Damascus Ghutah, Balkh River,[5] and Ubullah River;[6] and the fruit gardens of the world are three: al-Ubullah, Siraf and 'Uman."[7] The highly cultured poet abu-Bakr Muhammad ibn-al-'Abbas al-Khwarizmi said, "the earthly paradises are four: the Ghutah of Damascus, the Vale of Sughd near Samarqand, the Vale of Bawwan[8] and the Islet of Ubullah. I have seen them all and found Ghutah the best." According to ancient records, Abraham, peace be upon him, was born in the Ghutah of Damascus in a village called Barzah on Mt. Qasiyun. It is reported that the Prophet, Allah's blessing and peace be upon him, said, "When 'Isa [Jesus] returns he will land near the white minaret on the east side of Damascus."[9]

Damascus is the paradise of the east and the rising place of its radiant beauty. It was the last of the cities of Islam whose hospitality we enjoyed, and the bride of the towns we saw. We found it adorned with flowers of fragrant plants, displaying silk-brocaded garments in the form of gardens. The position it holds in the realm of beauty is firmly established; sumptuously ornamented she sits on her bridal throne.

The city was highly honored when Allah, extolled is He, gave refuge therein to the Messiah and his Mother, Allah's blessing and peace be upon both, "on an elevated spot, secure and abundant in water." Its umbrage is thick; its water tastes like that of the river in Paradise; its rivulets twist snake-like in all directions; its orchards generate gentle

---

4. A celebrated philologist, died 828.

5. The river, now dry, takes its name from the city Balkh, Greek Bactria, in what is today Afghanistan.

6. A canal from the Tigris to Basrah and southeast to the Persian Gulf.

7. Siraf on the eastern shore of the Persian Gulf; 'Uman in southeast Arabia.

8. In southwest Persia.

9. Yaqut, vol. II, p. 589. The white minaret still stands on the city wall near the east gate.

zephyr injecting life into souls. Before onlookers she arrays herself like a bride calling them: "Come on to a bridal place and linger."

So much water has the soil of Damascus absorbed that it got sick of it and yearns for thirst. Its solid stones almost cry out to you, "Run barefooted; here is a cool spot for washing and for drinking" (sur. 38: 41). The gardens of the city surround it like a halo around the moon; they contain it as a calyx contains a flower. Its verdant Ghutah stretches eastward as far as the eye can see; in fact wherever you look in all four directions, its bright, green foliage, laden with ripe fruit, holds your gaze. By Allah, they told the truth who said, "If Paradise be on earth, Damascus must be it; if it is in heaven, Damascus can parallel and match it."[10]

Damascus the fragrant, the oldest continually inhabited town known to history, beauty queen among Moslem cities and one of three paradises on earth, capital of the Umayyad dynasty, was for a time mistress of an empire greater than that of Rome at its height.

10. Ibn-Jubayr, pp. 234–235; cf. Broadhurst, pp. 271–272. This Spanish Moslem traveler visited Damascus in July 1184.

4
Baghdad: The Intellectual Capital

Among the cities of the world Baghdad stands out as the professor of the community of Islam.

Yaqut

Unlike its three predecessors Baghdad was a purely Arab creation. The name does not suggest Arabic etymology, but the pre-Islamic Persian or Aramaean settlement left no noteworthy political or commercial record. It was the 'Abbasid-built Baghdad that figured in history.

The region around Baghdad saw the rise and fall of more capital cities than perhaps any region of comparable size. Here flourished the earliest ones known to history, the Sumerian city states, such as Uruk, the Erech of Genesis 10:10. These were the cradle of our civilization. They were followed by Agade (Accad of Gen. 10:10), capital of Sargon, the first known Semitic monarch, and by Babylon, seat of Hammurabi and Nebuchadnezzar. A successor of Alexander the Great founded twenty miles southeast of the Baghdad site a city named after him to serve as capital of the eastern wing of his kingdom. Opposite Seleucia on the east bank of the Tigris rose Ctesiphon, capital of the ancient kingdom of Parthia and of Sasanid Persia. The Arab capital can be said to have fallen heir to all these capitals, outshone them all, and outlived them.

Such a rash on the face of a limited area must have been conditioned by special geopolitical factors. The alluvial plain between the Tigris and the Euphrates — where at Baghdad it is no more than thirty-three miles wide — is one of the best irrigated and most fertile in western Asia. Legend could not find a better place to locate its Garden of Eden. The twin rivers provided facile communication northward to the hinterland, southward to the Persian Gulf, and therefrom to other seas east and west. The position of the region between the Perso-Indian and Turkish lands on one hand, and the Semitic and Hamitic lands on the other made of it an international connecting bridge.

But the 'Abbasids had more personal reasons for transferring the seat of government from Syria to Iraq. The Iraqis formed the hard core of the anti-Umayyad movement. They were the first to proclaim abu-al-'Abbas as caliph. The spark that ignited the uprising was lit in Khurasan, eastern Persia. Moreover Moslem conquests in central Asia had shifted the center of gravity eastward, leaving the double capital of Arabia, as well as that of Syria, out of focus. It should also be remembered that while the Umayyads were for a time preoccupied with the idea of fighting Byzantium, the 'Abbasids adopted the principle of coexistence. Only once in their long history did the 'Abbasids make a serious attempt at Constantinople. This was in 782 when the third caliph al-Mahdi sent his second son, Harun, at the head of an army that reached Scutari (ancient Chrysopolis) opposite the Byzantine capital. Harun exacted from Irene, regent in the name of her son Constantine VI, a treaty stipulating the payment of an annual tribute of about 90,000 dinars. The feat won for Harun the honorific title of al-Rashid (the right-path follower), by which he became known, but so far as permanent results were concerned the campaign did not differ from its Umayyad antecedents. Harun's army was the last Arab one to cast covetous eyes on the walled city on the Bosporus.

I

It was not the first but the second 'Abbasid, al-Mansur (754–775), abu-al-'Abbas' brother and successor, who built the city that became the capital of the dynasty. The founder of this enduring monument was also the father of the dynasty, all thirty-five successors having been his lineal descendants. Unlike its three predecessors Baghdad came into existence by the elaborate act of one man.

Before deciding on the site the caliph canvassed other places and

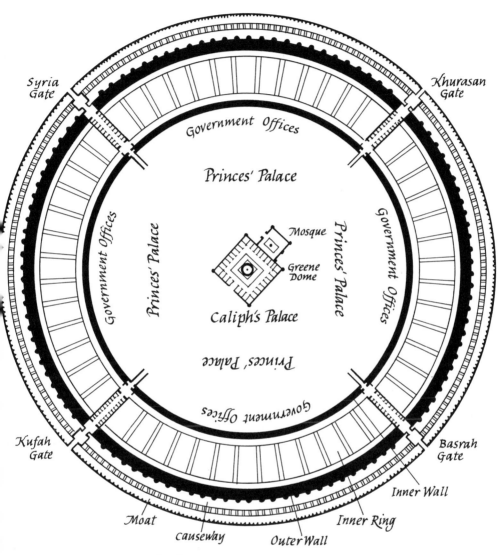

Plan of the Round City of Al-Mansur

Within the figure:
- Syria Gate
- Khurasan Gate
- Government Offices
- Princes' Palace
- Government Offices
- Princes' Palace
- Mosque
- Greene Dome
- Princes' Palace
- Caliph's Palace
- Government Offices
- Princes' Palace
- Kufah Gate
- Basrah Gate
- Inner Wall
- Moat
- Causeway
- Outer Wall
- Inner Ring

consulted advisers. His final choice was prompted by the following considerations as expressed by him:

This is an excellent place for a military camp. Here is the Tigris to keep us in touch with lands as far as China and bring us all that the seas yield. It will also give us the food products of Mesopotamia, Armenia and their adjacent territories. And there is the Euphrates to carry for us all that Syria, Raqqah and their adjacent territories have to offer.[1]

The caliph laid the first brick with his own hand on the west bank of the Tigris. He employed 100,000 architects, artisans, smiths, carpenters, and other laborers, requisitioned from different parts of the empire. For four years (762–766) they labored at a cost of 4,883,000 dirhams. The plan was unique in Moslem city architecture, perhaps inspired by the sight of the remains of Babylon and Ctesiphon and dictated by the desire for privacy and personal safety. The caliph had it all worked out in detail in ashes. The new town was centered on a circular nucleus comprising the caliphal palace and mosque, residences for the caliph's children, and government buildings. Some of the building material was quarried from the Ctesiphon ruins. The main palace covered an eighth of a mile, and housed the caliph, his wives, concubines, and slaves as well as his Khurasanian bodyguard. It also provided offices for secretaries and aides and reception halls for entertaining ambassadors, theologians, scholars, and other distinguished visitors. Because of its gilded entrance the palace became known as the Golden Gate. The hall ceilings took the form of domes, the highest of which was green in color and 130 feet high, giving it a wide-range visibility from all sides. Legend topped it with the figure of a mounted warrior holding a lance to point out the direction from which an enemy approached. The mosque adjoined the palace.

Al-Mansur surrounded his creation with a double wall and a water-filled moat. The wall rose to a height of 90 feet and was provided with inclined pathways to enable horsemen to reach the top which was about 40 feet wide. Four equidistant gateways pierced the wall, each high enough to allow the passage of a horseman holding aloft his lance. So heavy were the iron doors that they required a company of doormen to handle them. The city was given by its builder the official

1. Al-Tabari, *Ta'rikh al-Rusul w-al-Muluk*, ed. de Goeje et al. (Leyden, 1879–1901), vol. III, p. 272.

title of Dar al-Salam (the abode of peace), but on account of its shape it was popularly referred to as the Round City. Poetically it is referred to as al-Zawra' (the winding city) because of its location on the winding Tigris shore.

Among those consulted on the site was the court astrologer, who assured his royal patron that the horoscope was auspicious. It certainly was. In no time the area around the Round City mushroomed with buildings, mosques, and public baths supplied with water from river canals opened in Babylonian days and now renovated and extended. Al-Mansur's son and successor al-Mahdi erected a new palace on the east side of the Tigris. Before long the new quarter that developed around it vied with that on the west in size and affluence. In less than two generations, and as if by a magic wand, the old site of a Persian hamlet grew into a center of international importance politically and commercially. It became second to none in that part of the world except Constantinople. Indeed in one respect, the intellectual, Baghdad excelled its older rival. Meantime it served as a capital for the longest-lived (750–1258) and most celebrated of all Arab dynasties.

The transfer of the government seat from Damascus to Baghdad involved more than geography. It had political, social, and economic aspects.

Damascus had a window open on the west; Baghdad's window opened to the east. The new location exposed the new capital to fresh ideas and influences, mainly Persian. The Damascus regime had its power anchored in Syria and its desert, where South Arabians were domiciled. The Baghdad regime derived its power primarily from Iraqis and Persians. Baghdad in due course became more Persianized than Damascus was ever Syrianized. Its court followed that of the Khusraus. Persian wives, concubines, and wines became fashionable. Of the thirty-seven 'Abbasid caliphs only one had both parents of the Prophet's tribe. Al-Mansur was the first to adopt the Persian headgear and was naturally followed by courtiers and others down along the line.

The entire social structure in Baghdad underwent radical change. The tribal organization was virtually obliterated. The Arabian aristocracy based on blood — now adulterated — and on sword — now blunted — gave way to one of Neo-Moslems. A new social class of businessmen, merchants, craftsmen, theologians, and scholars arose. The Mediterranean fleet fell into disuse. A merchant marine in the Persian Gulf emerged. Trade assumed international proportions, products from all parts of the caliphate found their way into the bazars of the capital. Amidst this cycle of changes only two institutions held their own: religion and language. Islam continued to be the official religion of the state, and Arabic remained its language.

Conspicuous among the political institutions developed in the new capital was the vizirate. The father of the first vizirial family was Khalid ibn-Barmak, son of a Persian priest in a Buddhist monastery at Balkh. Khalid began his career as chief of the army and the land-tax bureau under abu-al-'Abbas al-Saffah and was later promoted to higher positions including the governorship of Tabaristan and Khurasan. Both al-Saffah and al-Mansur were impressed by his wise counsel, administrative ability, and military achievement. In his work Khalid was assisted by his son Yahya. The third caliph al-Mahdi (775–785) entrusted Yahya with the education of his son Harun. On his assumption of power in 786 Harun not only appointed Yahya as vizir but delegated to him unrestricted powers symbolized by passing on to him his personal seal. The caliph respectfully called him "father." Assisted by his two sons, al-Fadl and Ja'far, Yahya practically ruled the empire for seventeen years (786–803), a period known to historians as that of the Barmakid reign.

Meantime al-Fadl served as tutor for al-Amin, and Ja'far for al-Ma'mun, heirs apparent to the throne. Ja'far established such a reputation for eloquence, literary ability, and elegant penmanship that tradition credited him with founding the class of "people of the pen," in opposition to "people of the sword." His intimacy with the caliph was suspected of being of more than the ordinary character. The three Barmakids patronized science and art. They amassed fabulous fortunes, opened canals in the realm, erected mosques and other public buildings, and spent lavishly to win friends and eliminate enemies. A special creation of theirs was the bureau of poetry specializing in bestowing largesses on worthy panegyrists. Their sumptuous palaces on the east side of the capital became scenes of assemblies and banquets whose stories found their way into the *Arabian Nights*.

In January 803 the caliph, as if from a clear sky, had the thirty-seven–year–old Ja'far executed. His severed head was exhibited on a bridge and the two halves of his bisected body on two other bridges, there to remain for a year. His aged father and his brother died in prison. The Barmakid property in the amount of 30,676,000 dinars was confiscated. Ja'far's palace became the residence of Caliph al-Ma'mun. The vizirial family was wiped out of existence, but the vizirate continued and its incumbents under al-Ma'mun belonged to its school. Likewise the Barmakid name survived to the present as a synonym of unbounded generosity.

In the absence of an official explanation of the reasons for the tragic ending of such a prominent family, several reasons — such as impiety, pro-'Alid or pro-Persian proclivities — have been offered with no supporting evidence. One plausible explanation is that the caliph at last could no more tolerate the vizirial tutelage which had become hereditary and assumed the aspects of being a state within the state. In Harun's caliphal firmament there was no room for more than one sun. But why mutilate poor Ja'far's body remains a mystery.

II

Fact and fiction combine to make the reigns of Harun al-Rashid (786–809) and his son al-Ma'mun (813–833) in Baghdad the most glorious period not only in Arab but in Moslem history. Political prestige, financial supremacy, and intellectual activity were the three features of the age.

Harun ascended the throne with the memory of having conducted four years earlier a military campaign that imposed a humiliating tribute on the enemy of Islam still fresh in his subjects' minds. In fact he was still collecting instalments on the tribute, and when in 806 Nicephorus I dared repudiate the treaty Harun addressed to him this scathing message:

> In the name of Allah, the merciful, the compassionate. From Harun, the commander of the believers, to Nicephorus, the dog of a Roman. Verily I have read your letter, O son of an infidel mother, as for the answer it shall be for your eye to see, never for your ear to hear.
>
> Salam.[2]

2. *Ibid.*, p. 696.

True to his word, the caliph rushed a series of campaigns which ravaged as they penetrated deep into the enemy's territory. They ended in the imposition — additional to the tribute — of a tax on the emperor and members of his household. The event marks the highest point ever reached by 'Abbasid power.

At that time, early ninth century, only two names stood out in world affairs: Harun and Charlemagne. Western tradition credits them with exchanging embassies and gifts. That they had common interests is evident. Charlemagne could use the caliph as an ally against his Byzantine rival for supremacy in Christendom, and the caliph could use a Western friend against the emerging Umayyad power in Cordova. It was this reputed Harun-Charlemagne relation that, before translation of the *Arabian Nights*, made "the king of Persia, Aaron," for a time known in West Europe.

The growth of wealth in Baghdad kept pace with the growth of power. Business, industry, and trade took long strides forward. Basrah to the south at the juncture of the twin rivers, and Siraf on the Persian Gulf shared in the activity and the boom. All three ports carried on national and international trade by caravan and ship. The wharves of the capital city were dotted with ships of war, pleasure craft, merchant vessels, Chinese junks, and rafts of inflated sheepskins, ancestors of those still floated down the river. The carriers stocked the bazars of the city with rice, wheat, and linen from Egypt, glassware from Lebanon, fruits from Syria, pearls and weapons from Arabia, minerals and dyes from India, perfumes and rugs from Persia, silk and musk from China, fabrics and slaves from central Asia, ivory and black slaves from Africa. The hoards of 'Abbasid coins recently unearthed in places as remote as Scandinavia testify to the worldwide commercial activity of this and later periods. The fantastic adventures of Sinbad (Sindbad) and other *Arabian Nights* tales must have had a basis in actual reports of Moslem voyagers.

Records of the huge fortunes amassed by the tycoons of the day sound like those of the multimillionaires of modern industry. The confiscated property of one of these tycoons by Harun was in the amount of 50,000,000 dirhams in cash plus a daily income of 100,000 dirhams from real estate. A special "bureau of confiscation" was later created to handle cases of officials who fell from grace or of private citizens whose wealth aroused caliphal cupidity. The estate of Harun's mother yielded an income of 160,000,000 dirhams as reported by no less an authority than the historian al-Mas'udi, who spells out the figures ("a hundred thousand thousand and sixty thousand thousand").

The state revenue, of course, followed the upward curve of the national income. The main sources were alms-tax from Moslems, poll- and land-tax from non-Moslems, duty on imports by non-Moslems, ransom for prisoners of war, and tribute from foreign enemies. From the varying estimates that have come down to us, it may be safe to assume that in this period the state revenue from all provinces in cash and in kind reached an all-time high of some 330,000,000 dirhams. On Harun's death the state treasury contained, if we can believe al-Tabari, dean of Arab historians, 900,000,000 dinars.

The scale on which Harun and his two immediate successors lived was unprecedented in caliphal history. Harun's princely munificence endeared him to historians. It attracted poets and scholars, musicians and dancers, wits and jesters, boon companions, trainers of fighting dogs and cocks from all over the realm. The favorite poet was abu-Nuwas, son of a Persian washerwoman and a specialist in erotic and bacchanalian compositions. Of his love of boys, abu-Nuwas made no secret in his poetry. He served as a boon companion to al-Amin, Harun's son and successor for an interval of four years (809–813). The roster of singer-musicians was headed by Ibrahim al-Mawsili, born in Mosul to a Persian family and credited with being the first in Arab history "to beat the rhythm with a wand." Ibrahim, chroniclers report, received a monthly salary of 10,000 dirhams plus bonuses for especially pleasing single performances. In one such case he was rewarded by his patron in the amount of 100,000 dirhams.

Harun's cousin-wife Zubaydah set the style for the smart set. When she ornamented her shoes with precious stones, they followed. At her table the first lady of the land would tolerate no vessels but those of gold and silver studded with gems. Many others of the caliphal family could well afford it. Members of the Prophet's tribe were still receiving mounting subsidies from the state treasury as initiated by 'Umar ibn-al-Khattab. A brother of Harun once offered him at a banquet a dish of 150 fish tongues at a cost of 1,000 dirhams. Ceremonial occasions furnished themes for a variety of fantastic reports. Among these extravaganzas that of al-Ma'mun's wedding in 825 to the eighteen-year-old Buran, daughter of one of his governors, stands out as an unforgettable one. The royal couple sat on a golden mat studded with sapphires. Candles of ambergris turned the night into day. The ladies of the court, resplendent in their attire, were headed by Zubaydah. The poets were there to sing and memorialize the occasion in verse. The bridal shower consisted of a thousand pearls of unique size. Distinguished guests received musk balls each containing a slave, a piece of property, or some other valuable gift. The rest were given gold or silver coins.

The real glory that was Baghdad, however, lay not so much in the field of might or wealth as in that of intellect and creativity. In the first hundred years of its existence the 'Abbasid capital, particularly during the reigns of Harun and al-Ma'mun, attained supremacy in intellectual as it did in material endeavor and achievement. While the scholars of its neighbors Basrah and Kufah were laying the foundations of the principal purely Arab sciences — koranic, linguistic, historical, theological, legal — the Baghdad scholars were delving into what they termed the sciences of the ancients — mathematics, astronomy, medicine, and philosophy — the ancients being Persians, Indians, and above all Greeks. This activity of the mind in Baghdad passed through two stages, translation and origination, not mutually exclusive. Certain translators engaged also in research work and made original contributions. The translation movement was initiated by al-Mansur and culminated under al-Ma'mun. It did not cease until the richest treasures of Greek thought were rendered available in the language of the Koran. No such experience did the Arabic-speaking world pass through until the nineteenth century, when French and English took the place of Greek. In Europe it reminds us of the Renaissance of the sixteenth century.

The period of origination centered in Baghdad began under Harun and al-Ma'mun and lasted for more than a century. It made of the Arab capital a world scientific center comparable to that of Rome in law, Athens in philosophy, and Jerusalem in religion. Radiation reached the farthest limits of the eastern caliphate and was relayed into the western caliphate of Cordova, whence it continued to spread till the end of the twelfth century. Origination was followed by a period of transmission based mainly in Toledo, in the course of which Moslem scientific and philosophic contributions were made available to medieval Christendom. Thus did the Baghdad heritage become a part of world heritage.

The translation movement had its start in two manuscripts, one mathematical and the other astronomical, brought into the court of al-Mansur from India. Their Arabic rendition introduced these two sciences into the world of Islam. Of perhaps no less importance was their introduction of what Europeans call Arabic numerals and the Arabs Hindi numerals. The zero (from Ar. *sifr*, meaning "empty") may have been an Arab invention. In due course the new system replaced the alphabetic one current in both East and West. Without it the measure of progress in the mathematical sciences since then would have been inconceivable.

Another translational achievement of al-Mansur was in the literary field. It involved rendering into Arabic by his Persian secretary ibn-al-Muqaffa' of a collection of delightful short stories. The Persian text had an Indian origin. The stories are put in the mouth of animals and intended to instruct the reader in the proper conduct. The narrator is an Indian philosopher named Bidpai, hence the English title *Bidpai Fables*. The Arabic title is *Kalilah wa-Dimnah*. So successful was ibn-al-Muqaffa''s translation — in fact it was an adaptation — that his edition, the first literary work in Arabic, soon established itself as a classic and served as a model for later works. It is still used as a textbook in elementary schools. It made of ibn-al-Muqaffa' a father of Arabic secular literary prose paralleling Muhammad as the father of religious prose. What gives the Arabic version added international importance is the fact that because of the loss of the Persian the Arabic served as the original for numberless translations into European and Asian languages.

Another and better-known collection of fairy tales and other stories of ultimate Perso-Indian is *Alf Laylah wa-Laylah* (a thousand and one nights, commonly referred to as *Arabian Nights*). The *Nights* had its source in a Persian work (*Hazar Afsana*, thousand tales) comprising stories again of Indian origin. The translation was done in Baghdad before the mid-tenth century and was enlarged into a recension enriched with anecdotes about the 'Abbasid court and its subjects. The story of Sinbad the Sailor, among others, seems to have taken its shape in this city. The frame-story enclosing the entire collection originated in India.

If the Persians mediated Indian lore to the Arabs, the Syrians (Suryan, Syriac speakers) mediated Greek lore. Syria, it should be recalled, had been exposed to Greek cultural influences for a thousand years before the advent of Islam. By this time the educated among its people were studying and using Greek as their successors in Iraq, Syria, Lebanon, and Palestine are doing today with French and English.

Among the non-Christian Syrians was a community of star-worshipers in Harran, whose scholars specialized in Greek astronomy. One of them al-Hajjaj ibn-Matar is credited with the translation (829) of Ptolemy's *Megale Syntaxis* (the great construction) of astronomy under the title of *al-Majusti*. Ptolemy was a Greek Alexandrian who flourished about A.D. 140. The Ptolemaic system made the sun, planets, and stars revolve round the earth. It was universally accepted until the seventeenth century, when it was superseded by the Copernican system. The Greek original of the book was lost and the Arabic in the form of *Almagest* served as source for all surviving editions. Al-Hajjaj also made an Arabic translation of the *Elements* of Euclid, the renowned Greek geometer who also flourished in Alexandria (ca. 300 B.C.). The translator evidently prepared two versions, one for Harun and the other for al-Ma'mun. Euclid's book became the source of geometrical knowledge in the East as it was in the West, and in its revisions it is still used as a text. Baghdad's interest in astronomy stemmed from the then general belief in the influence of the stars upon human affairs and in the ability to foretell terrestrial events by the stars' positions and aspects. All the caliphs had their astrologers.

Al-Hajjaj was the forerunner of a series of distinguished Harranian scholars in the service of the Baghdad court. The most productive among them was Thabit ibn-Qurrah (ca. 836–901) who found in Caliph al-Mu'tadid (892–902) not only a patron but a personal friend and a table host. Thabit's school included his son, two grandsons, and a great-grandson and was responsible for revising old translations, such as that of Euclid, and undertaking new ones, covering the bulk of Greek astronomical and mathematical writings. Included among the translated works were those of the celebrated Sicilian-Greek mathematician and inventor Archimedes (d. 212 B.C.), credited with the discovery of the principle that a body immersed in a fluid loses as much in weight as the weight of an equal volume of the fluid.

Christian Syrians were no less interested in the cultivation of Hellenistic studies than their heathen countrymen. They specialized in philosophical and medical subjects. Their clergy were not slow to detect the importance of understanding the theology of Greek Church Fathers and the value of the use of logical methods in their polemics with members of other sects. As early as the fourth century they began in monasteries to translate into Syriac, a sister of Arabic. Certain Greek Christian concepts were couched in philosophical terms, setting a precedent for Syrian theology. In the Hellenistic tradition philosophy and medicine were closely associated, and the study of one normally involved the other.

The leading philosophical school in the area at the rise of Islam was that of Alexandria. The Moslem conquest severed this school's connection with Byzantium and forced its removal (ca. 718) into Antioch. From Antioch it migrated eastward to Harran and landed ultimately in the 'Abbasid metropolis. Transferring schools in those days meant no more than moving professors and their books. The leading medical school was that of Jundaysabur (western Persia), where Indian and Greek traditions met and Nestorian professors prevailed. The school supplied the caliphs, beginning with al-Mansur, with court physicians for more than a hundred years. The series was led by Jurjis (George) ibn-Bakhtishu', whose son Jibril (Gabriel) built for Harun in Baghdad a hospital modeled after that of Jundaysabur. Six or seven Bakhtishu' generations carried on the medical tradition.

The shaykh of all translators was another Nestorian Hunayn (Joannitius) ibn-Ishaq (809–873). Hunayn studied medicine at Baghdad, traveled in Asia Minor in quest of manuscripts, and mastered Greek, Syriac, and Arabic. This scholar was fortunate in receiving the munificent patronage of al-Ma'mun and after him al-Mutawakkil (847–861), whose court physician he was. Al-Ma'mun appointed Hunayn as dean of his newly built Bayt al-Hikmah (house of wisdom), a remarkable ensemble of library, bureau of translation, copying manuscripts, and scientific research. Al-Ma'mun's interest stemmed from the fact that he had adopted the Mu'tazili view of the creation of the Koran and sought in philosophy justification for this and other radical views. The Mu'tazilah argued that the dogma of the uncreated character of the Koran compromised God's unity, the cornerstone of Islamic belief. They later taught the doctrine of free will — a reflex of Greek philosophy — arguing that God's justice requires it, otherwise man becomes irresponsible for his act. Hence their name for themselves: People of Unity and Justice.

The caliph is said to have paid Hunayn in gold the weight of the books he rendered into Arabic. Assisted by his son and nephew, the dean of Bayt al-Hikmah revised earlier translations and prepared new ones of Galen, Hippocrates, and Dioscorides in medicine as well as other works by Plato and Aristotle in philosophy. A recently published book ascribed to Hunayn makes him the author of the earliest extant systematic text of ophthalmology.

The era of creative work followed that of Arabizing Indian and Greek science and philosophy. Its exponents were Moslems of the "neo-" type. This period of origination involved mathematical, astronomical, and geographical sciences, medicine, pharmacopoeia and botany, music, logic, metaphysics, and other disciplines then considered branches of philosophy. Transmission into Europe was conducted through Latin by Western Christians — with Jews collaborating — and followed three routes: Crusading Syria, Moslem Sicily, and Moslem Spain.

The earliest scientist was Muhammad ibn-Musa al-Khwarizmi, whose second surname al-Majusi (Magian) attests to his Zoroastrian ancestry. Al-Khwarizmi flourished in the court of al-Ma'mun. He made his starting point research in the two manuscripts from India. The set of astronomical tables (*zij*) he drew was the first of its kind in Islam. Revised about two and a half centuries later by his coreligionist in Spain al-Majriti (of Madrid), al-Khwarizmi's zij found its way (1126) into Latin — thanks to the efforts of Adelard of Bath — to serve as a basis for later planetary tables in the languages of Europe as it had done in those of Asia as far as China. Al-Majriti's recension had a trigonometric supplement in which the term *jayb* (pocket) was used and was translated into "sine," adding a new technical term to European languages. Regrettably, the Arabic original of this early work has been lost, but its Latin translation survived and has been as late as a few years ago put into English and published. Al-Khwarizmi further prepared, perhaps in collaboration with other scholars, for his patron an atlas of the maps of heaven of which the text accompanying the maps has been preserved.

This early scholar was the father not only of astronomy but of mathematics, too. His claim to fame here rests primarily on *Hisab al-Jabr w-al-Muqabalah* (algebraic calculations and equations), composed in response to his patron's request to produce a simplified presentation of mathematical science and to add material relating to land survey and inheritance division. Al-Khwarizmi's *al-Jabr* was translated into Latin in 1143 by another Englishman, Robert of Chester, in Toledo, Spain. Here a school of translation, initiated by Archbishop Raymond (1126–1151) flourished for over a century, beginning about 1135. The most prolific of the Toledan translators was an Italian, Gerard of Cremona, the opposite number in the West of Hunayn ibn-Ishaq. Gerard made another Latin rendition of *al-Jabr* and translated Euclid's *Elements*, a version of Ptolemy's *Almagest*, various philosophical treatises headed by those of Aristotle, and the medical works of Galen and Hippocrates — in all seventy-one books. The translation of al-Khwarizmi's mathematical works was responsible for introducing the Arabic numerals into the West. These numerals became known after him as algorisms, a term used also in the sense of arithmetic. Another zij of Arab authorship was done into Spanish under the auspices of Alfonso the Wise of Castile and Leon (1252–1284) and was later passed on into Latin. Alfonso was also responsible for a Spanish rendition of the *Bidpai Fables*.

Arab contributions in philosophy may not seem so original as those in science, but that does not mean they were of no importance. Largely relating to the marginal zone where religion and philosophy meet, they involved harmonizing the products of faith with those of reason, in other words, reconciling truths arrived at by theology with those arrived at by philosophy — a seemingly impossible assignment. Arab scholars in Baghdad and al-Andalus (to use their name for Moslem Spain) endeavored to keep one foot in Mecca and Medina while reaching with the other into Athens and Alexandria. To the extent to which their efforts were successful they enriched Islamic as well as Christian religious thought, and contributed substantially to the universal stream of liberalism.

The philosophy which interested them was not so much that of Plato and Aristotle as of its later, Neoplatonic version. Neoplatonism was a syncretistic system with a religious overtone which the older system lacked. It adopted Platonic metaphysics, Aristotelian philosophical method, Stoic ethics, Pythagorean concepts as well as Near Eastern mystical and gnostic elements. Its center was Alexandria of the fourth and fifth Christian centuries. Its founders and exponents included two Near Easterners: Porphyry (purple-clad, also known as Malchus, from Semitic Melik, king, d. ca. 304) and Iamblichus (d. ca. 333). Porphyry was born in Batanaea (Syria) or Tyre (Lebanon). He emphasized the element of asceticism for soul purification. His follower Iamblichus, born in Chalcis (today 'Anjar in Lebanon), adopted the Neopythagorean system ascribing to numbers a metaphysical value higher than the mathematical. The so-called *Theology of Aristotle*, which was avidly studied by Moslems, was a spurious work authored by a Neoplatonist. To Moslem thinkers, as to the Eastern Christian thinkers before them, Neoplatonism was obviously more congenial than early Greek philosophy.

The first Arab philosopher was al-Kindi (abu-Yusuf Ya'qub, ca. 801–873), scion of a royal Yamani family domiciled at Kufah, where his father and grandfather had served as governors. Known to his countrymen as Faylasuf al-'Arab (philosopher of the Arabs), al-Kindi was not only the first philosopher of Arab descent but the only major one. On joining the galaxy of intellectuals in the Baghdad court the young scholar was already inoculated with Mu'tazili liberal views. Not satisfied with the available translations of Greek philosophical works, he had the Neoplatonic *Theology of Aristotle* especially done into Arabic for his use by a Christian Syrian from Hims. This he used as a text for instructing his pupil Ahmad, son of al-Mu'tasim (833–842). Al-Mu'tasim was brother and successor of al-Ma'mun.

In an early work titled *Risalah fi al-Falsafah al-'Ula* (epistle on the first philosophy) the budding philosopher started on a high note, ranking philosophy as the highest of all activities and defining it as "knowledge of things as they are in reality, insofar as human ability can determine." This put philosophy above theology and its subsidiary sciences of jurisprudence and ethics and put the author deep in trouble. It raised vexatious and perplexing problems. Resort was made to explanations. In the case of philosophy, he argued, conclusions are drawn by rational reasoning and logical procedure and are subject to demonstration; in the case of religion conclusions are drawn by Prophetic intuition and spontaneous methods requiring no research and are acceptable by faith. The results, however, are not necessarily contradictory. Al-Kindi thereby opened the way for the existence of a two-level truth: one for the intellectual elite and the other for the masses.

But such argumentation did not impress the ulama. Aristotle taught that matter is ancient and creation cannot be from nothing; the Koran taught that "all He needs to do, when He wishes a thing, is to say to it 'Be' and it is" (36:82). No philosopher could, by any process of rational reasoning, accept the resurrection of the body, but the Koran is explicit and subjects the body in future life to physical pains and pleasures:

Verily, we have prepared for the unbelievers chains and fetters and a blazing fire. Verily, the righteous will drink of a cup of which the admixture is camphor; a spring at which the servants of Allah drink, making it bubble up abundantly.

76:4–6

But al-Kindi had an explanation, an explanation which, elaborated by later Moslem philosophers, led to the belief in a double standard of veracity. Prophets use rhetorical phraseology and the kind of language that appeals to the masses. Sensuous pleasures appeal to the common, but the intellectual is more interested in spiritual pleasures. When a successor of al-Kindi, ibn-Sina (Avicenna, d. 1037), was reminded that wine, to which he was addicted, was prohibited in the Koran, his reply was: "Religious law makes drinking illegal for the ignorant, but intelligence makes it legal for the intellectual."

Al-Kindi made another contribution to scriptural exegesis. In the course of a session on the Koran, his puzzled royal pupil raised a question about the exact meaning of a passage reading: "The stars and the trees offer worship" (55:6; in another passage, 22:18, the sun, moon, mountains, and beasts are added). "Worship" in such cases, explained the tutor, should not be taken in its literal sense. It simply means follow laws ordained by their Creator. Al-Kindi thereby opened the way for allegorical interpretation of koranic material, a device that has not ceased to the present day to render service to liberal reformers.

101

BAGHDAD

More than a philosopher, the first Arab philosopher was a physician, a musician, a mathematician, and an astrologer. He served as court physician to the caliphs under whom he flourished and authored thirty-six extant treatises on the subject. He is said to have cured the paralyzed son of a neighbor — who had been given up by Baghdadi practitioners — by the use of music. Of the fifteen works on music, only five have survived. In the title of one he uses the term *musiqi*, presumably for the first time in an Arabic book title. His book on optics (*al-Manazir*) was used in its Latin translation by the English scientist Roger Bacon (d. 1294). This with his other works on medicine and astrology done into Latin in Toledo made Alkindus' name familiar throughout Europe. A sixteenth-century Italian physician and mathematician counted Alkindus among the twelve greatest minds of history. In the millenary (according to the lunar calendar) anniversary held by Baghdad in 1962 for its philosopher, an orientalist read a paper listing 281 titles attributed to al-Kindi. Ironically, more of his works survived in Latin than in Arabic.

The names of two other philosophers are associated with that of Baghdad, one a Persian al-Razi (Lat. Rhazes, d. 925) and the other a Turk al-Farabi (Alpharabius, d. 950). Al-Razi was born in Rayy, outside of Teheran, as his name indicates. In common with other Moslem philosophers, he was also a physician having studied and practiced medicine in Baghdad. As head of the city hospital he chose a site for its building by suspending shreds of meat in different quarters and finding out where the least signs of putrefaction appeared — a device primitive to us but advanced in those days. His treatise on smallpox and measles (*al-Judari w-al-Hasbah*) was the first to distinguish clinically between these two diseases and has been translated into several European languages, including English. Al-Razi's originality was not shown in the medical field only. He stands unique among Moslem philosophers in rejecting all claims to validity by the teachings of the prophets — including Muhammad and Jesus — and insisting on the cultivation of philosophy and the use of reason as means for self-development. Of all philosophers Plato was his favorite.

Like al-Razi, al-Farabi studied in Baghdad but did not live there. His commentaries on Aristotle's works, particularly those on logic, physics, and metaphysics, established his reputation as the "second teacher" (*al-mu'allim al-thani*) after Aristotle. Al-Farabi was, moreover, responsible for introducing Plato into Islam as the supreme authority on political philosophy. Inspired by Plato's *Republic*, he wrote *Risalah fi Ara' Ahl al-Madinah al-Fadilah* (epistle on the opinions of the people of the superior city), in which he conceived of a model city as a hierarchical organism analogous to the human body and governed by wise men who see that all members behave in harmony and who prepare them to obtain felicity hereafter.

Baghdad cradled other disciplines more intimately related to Islam the religion. Three of the four founders of the orthodox schools of Islamic law lived and labored in it. Abu-Yusuf, a founder of the Hanafi school, the oldest and in certain respects the most liberal, was a judge in Harun's court. The eponym of the school, abu-Hanifah, a teacher of abu-Yusuf, left no books. He was buried in Baghdad (767), where his shrine, with its nine hundred–year–old dome, contributed to making the 'Abbasid capital a city of shrines. The third oldest school bears the name of al-Shafi'i (d. 820), who taught his specialty at Baghdad and laid the basis of the entire science of Islamic jurisprudence (*fiqh*). Ibn-Hanbal, founder of the fourth and most conservative school, today the official system of Su'udi Arabia, was born and buried (855) in Baghdad.

In theology, suffice it to mention al-Ghazzali (d. 1111), professor at the Nizamiyah model academy of Baghdad, one of the greatest religious thinkers in history and author of *Ihya' 'Ulum al-Din* (revivification of the sciences of religion), comparable in its influence to Thomas Aquinas' *Summa Theologiae*. The Nizamiyah derives its name from the enlightened Persian vizir Nizam-al-Mulk (d. 1092), an ornament in the Saljuq court. The first faternal order of Sufi (mystic) Islam was founded in Baghdad by 'Abd-al-Qadir al-Jilani (d. 1166). This Qadiri order, one of the most charitable and tolerant orders, served as a model for later ones. Even today it claims followers throughout the world of Islam. The founder's tomb, a rival in beauty to that of abu-Hanifah, is still the object of pilgrimage from near and far. In brief, hardly an intellectual movement appeared in early medieval Islam without Baghdad's sharing in it. Mecca was raised to greatness by the birth of the Prophet, Medina by the success of his mission and by his immediate successors' residence, but Baghdad achieved greatness by its learning.

BAGHDAD

The learned al-Shafi'i, who was born in Ghazzah (Gaza), educated in Mecca, and died in Cairo, expressed the feeling — a home all scholars had in Baghdad: "I have never entered a town which I did not consider just another place in a journey except Baghdad, for when I entered it I considered it my home." When a learned Buwayhid vizir returned home from a visit to Baghdad and was asked about it his impressions, his reply was: "Among the cities of the world Baghdad stands out as the professor of the community of Islam."[3]

III

Under Damascus the caliphal empire was coterminous with Islam; under Baghdad it was not. Six years after the establishment of the 'Abbasid caliphate in 750, its western extremity, Spain, was amputated to become an independent Umayyad rival and extend its sway into northwestern Africa. In 929 the Umayyad Sunnite sultan 'Abd-al-Rahman III proclaimed himself caliph. (His capital Cordova forms the subject of a later chapter.) By this time the centrifugal forces of the empire, involving tribalism, nationalism, dissatisfaction with the establishment, as well as personal ambitions, were in full swing. Of the five centuries of Baghdad's ascendancy only the first was of relative grandeur and prosperity. In 800 Harun sent to Qayrawan as governor a trusted lieutenant named Ibrahim ibn-al-Aghlab, who with his successors exercised virtual autonomy over their realm, extended it into Sicily and seldom bothered to inscribe the caliph's name on the coinage they struck. In 909 the Sunnite Aghlabids were replaced by the ultra-Shi'ite Fatimids, whose founder took an unprecedented step and proclaimed himself caliph. A later Fatimid built Cairo (to be treated in the next chapter) and in 973 made it his capital. For two centuries after that, Fatimid Cairo was a rival to Baghdad and at times posed a real threat.

While the wings of the 'Abbasid eagle were in the west being clipped by Arab hands, its wings in the east were receiving the same treatment at the hands of Persians and Turks. The procedure followed the same law: The power of a provincial governor varied in direct proportion to the distance from the caliphal seat, and in inverse proportion to the

---

3. Yaqut, vol. I, p. 686.

power exercised by its incumbent. In 820 al-Ma'mun entrusted his general Tahir, son of a Persian slave, with the governorship of Khurasan and Transoxiana. Tahir lost no time in deleting the caliph's name from the Friday prayer, acting independently, and passing the realm to his sons. The Tahirid was followed by two equally short-lived Persian dynasties. Finally the political power passed into the hands of Turks represented at the height of their power by Sultan Mahmud of Ghaznah in eastern Afghanistan. In the course of his reign (997–1030) Mahmud invaded India seventeen times and extended his domain from the Ganges to the Tigris and northward to the Oxus.

As the extremities of the caliphate were being amputated on both sides a dagger was pointed at its very heart. As a measure of self-protection al-Mu'tasim (833–842), instituted a bodyguard of Turkish slaves and mercenaries numbering about four thousand. So unbearable did the conduct of this military corps become to the populace that in 836 the caliph had to move his seat to Samarra sixty miles up the Tigris. There the caliphs made their residence for fifty-three years, as the capital's condition moved from bad to worse. In the meantime caliphal prestige had fallen so low that when in 945 a Shi'ite general named Ahmad ibn-Buwayh, claiming descent from the pre-Islamic Sasanid dynasty, advanced against Baghdad and installed himself in the seat of authority, he encountered no opposition. The helpless caliph obligingly bestowed on the intruder the title of Mu'izz-al-Dawlah (strength-giver to the state) and left him in charge of state affairs. Shorn of temporal power the caliphate maintained what could be called spiritual power, suffering thereby its deepest humiliation and darkest eclipse. A new page was turned in 1055 but it was in the same chapter. A Turkish leader by the name Tughril Beg, grandson of Saljuq, appeared at the head of his Turkoman hordes and was received by the puppet caliph as a deliverer. The new master was at least a Sunnite. The Saljuq dynasty, rather dynasties, proved to be more powerful and more enduring than any of their predecessors. They rejuvenated the Moslem society, reunited Moslem western Asia, extended their rule into western Asia Minor, dealt the first blows to the Crusaders, and paved the way for the rise of the Ottoman dynasty.

Finally a new danger loomed in the eastern horizon. Mounted on fleet horses, armed with strange bows, and intent upon sharing in the richer life to the west of them, Mongolian hordes under Chingiz Khan swept in 1218 to 1222 from China through central Asia, leaving a trail of blood and devastation. The self-styled "scourge of God" behaved in style. Khwarizm, Bukhara, Samarqand, Balkh, and other centers of Islam were left in ruins. But that was a prelude. In 1256 a grandson of Chingiz named Hulagu pushed on the conquests reaching Alamut, nest of the Assassins on the Caspian shore. Two years later the mangonels of the Mongol invader were battering the Baghdad walls. By this time the 'Abbasid senile decay had reached the point of hopelessness. Caliph al-Musta'in (1242–1258) rushed a delegation to offer unconditional surrender but Hulagu would not receive it. On February 10 his men opened a breach in the wall, swarmed into the city, and began the slaughter. The entire caliphal family, together with three hundred court officials, were wiped out of existence. Parts of the city were plundered, others set ablaze. Mosques, shrines, schools, libraries, and other monumental structures were forever lost. Books that did not burn were thrown into the Tigris, whose water, we are told, ran black for days. The indiscriminate one-week slaughter, chroniclers claim, left 700,000 victims, which may have been 70,000, including refugees from the environs. The streets were strewn with corpses that emitted odors for days, forcing the invaders to evacuate the town for a time. Happily by this time the basic disciplines of Islamic culture, involving religion, language, science, and philosophy, had been not only firmly established but disseminated through North Africa to Spain, and through India and Turkestan to the borders of China. But the home of those disciplines was no more. The five hundred–year–old capital passed into oblivion, not to rise again for another seven hundred years.

IV

The defunct capital joined the sisterhood of forgotten cities but under special handicaps. Damascus enrolled as a virtually intact town. Mecca and Medina had self-rejuvenating forces in the pilgrimage. In the case of Baghdad, however, the destructive forces of flood and inundation, fire, riots, and looting — even Mongol invasions — continued to take their toll. So frequent were the Tigris' ruinous inundations that a modern Iraqi scholar devoted a three-volume study (*Fayadanat Baghdad*) to the subject. Sweeping waters from the river often left pools for germs to develop and added epidemics to the list. In his second campaign (1401) Timur (Tamerlane), a descendant of Chingiz Khan, put the Baghdadis indiscriminately to the sword. The surviving few fled or emigrated. Any public buildings spared by Hulagu were his victims. What was once Baghdad became a wasteland. His nickname Prince of Destruction was well deserved.

Of al-Mansur's abode of Peace, with its palaces, walls, and gates, hardly a trace was left. In fact its deterioration had begun early, in the civil war between the two brothers al-Amin and al-Ma'mun (811–813) and moved at a rapid pace. On the return of the caliphate from Samarra (889) the entire court was moved to the east bank of the river. Of the monumental 'Abbasid structures, al-Mustansiriyah is almost the only one left. Built in 1234 by the next-to-last caliph al-Mustansir for the four orthodox schools of jurisprudence, this institution had a hospital in which medicine was evidently taught. Theology always went with jurisprudence. As an educational institution it must have ranked next to the Nizamiyah. Renovated in 1961, it is today a chief attraction for visitors and sightseers.

Years before Chingiz' invasion the Andalusian traveler ibn-Jubayr found Baghdad (in 1184) a dilapidated town.

This old city still serves as the 'Abbasid capital and as the radiation center of the Hashimid Qurayshi imamate cause. But most of its substance is gone. Only the name remains. In comparison with its former self — prior to the assaults of misfortune and the concentration of adversity — the city is but a trace of a vanished encampment, a shadow of a passing ghost. No beauty is here to arrest the sight or to make a busy passer-by stop and gaze — unless it be the Tigris lying between its eastern and western quarters like a mirror shining between two panels, or a necklace ranged between two breasts. From it the city drinks and suffers no thirst, and into it she looks as into a mirror that tarnishes not. Between Baghdad's air and water Baghdad's feminine beauty develops, acquires reputation and becomes a subject of conversation all over the land. Against the perils of such seduction only Allah can offer protection.[4]

Among other sketches of life in the city ibn-Jubayr gives us a glimpse of the city's hospital and bathhouses:

The Suq al-Maristan [the hospital street] is a town in itself. In it the famous Baghdad Hospital stands, stretching on the Tigris bank. Its

4. Ibn-Jubayr, pp. 193–194; cf. Broadhurst, p. 226.

physicians make their rounds every Monday and Thursday to examine patients and prescribe for their needs. At the physicians' disposal are attendants who fill drug prescriptions and prepare food. The building is in fact a palace with bowers, chambers and all appurtenances of a royal dwelling. A conduit furnishes it with water from the Tigris.[5]

The bathhouses in the city are numberless, but according to one of its shaykhs they in the eastern and western quarters number two thousand. Most of them are faced with pitch that looks to a spectator like polished black marble. The majority of bathhouses in the region are so treated because of the abundance of available pitch. Strange is the story of this material! It is brought from a spring between Basrah and Kufah where Allah has caused to flow water that produces it. The pitch accumulates on the sides, clay-like, to be scooped, and after congealing, to be carried away. Glory to Allah Creator of whatever He willeth; no god but He.[6]

In Western Europe the fallen capital went the way of Ctesiphon onto the discarded pile of history. It was confused with Ctesiphon, Seleucia, and more often Babylon. Its name was corrupted almost beyond recognition.

The first European to describe the city after its downfall was the Venetian Marco Polo, the first man to blaze a trail across the Asian continent. In 1271 Marco, accompanied by his father and uncle, started on his long journey from Acre ('Akka). Strangely, this celebrated traveler calls the city Baudas. The seventeenth century yielded no improvement. In the 1620s, when the possession of Baghdad was contested by Safawid Persians and Ottoman Turks the British ambassador in Constantinople referred to Baghdad in his dispatches as "Babilon." In 1651 the French merchant and pioneer of trade with India Tavernier (Jean Baptiste) visited Baghdad, "qu'on appelle d'ordinaire Babylone," and estimated its population at 1,400. The map of the city he sketched did not radically differ from that drawn by the British on their occupation in 1917. A geography book published in Amsterdam in 1663 refers to the capital of "Chaldaea and Babylonia" "also called Baldach and Baudras by some." "Baldach," also "Baldacco," "Baldachino" gave us "baldachin," the rich brocade originally manufactured in Baghdad. It was not until the early eighteenth century that the capital of Harun al-Rashid sprang again into life thanks to Galland's

5. Ibn-Jubayr, p. 201; Broadhurst, pp. 234–235.

6. Ibn-Jubayr, pp. 204–205; Broadhurst, p. 238.

Modern Baghdad with the Republic's Square in foreground

translation of the *Arabian Nights* (*Mille et une nuits*). In the United States, however, in the mid-nineteenth century Longfellow was still writing in his "Spanish Jew's Tale" about "Baldacca's Kalif."[7]

In the East the memory of the old city continued to be cherished by writers and readers, but as a capital of importance it was not fully restored until Faysal, son of King Husayn of Hijaz, chose it in 1921 as the seat of his kingdom under the British mandate. It had served during the Ottoman period as capital of a province in Iraq. The monarchy was replaced in 1958 by a republic.

Baghdad the Winding City on the Tigris, metropolis of the world of Islam, capital of its most celebrated and longest-lived caliphate, scene of many Arabian Nights, home of Moslem theology and jurisprudence, Arab science and philosophy, was for centuries the intellectual center of Islam and for a time of the world.

7. Henry W. Longfellow, *Poetical Works* (Boston, 1874), p. 276.

109

5
Cairo:
The Dissident Capital

Misr, mother of the country, ex-seat of Pharoah the tyrant,
mistress of extensive provinces and fruitful territories,
boundless in the number of buildings, peerless in beauty
and splendor; the rendezvous of comers and goers and
the stopping place of the powerful and the powerless.

Ibn-Battutah

Cairo like Baghdad was an Arab foundation. But its founder stood at the other extremity of the Arab spectrum from Baghdad's founder. He was of Christian slave origin, whereas the other was a scion of the Prophet's tribe and his successor. The name leaves no doubt: Jawhar (jewel) al-Siqilli (the Sicilian) al-Rumi (the Greek). Arab masters named their slaves, especially if freed, after precious stones. The name of Yaqut al-Rumi meant sapphire. "Rumi" in this connection means Greek speaking.

Jawhar was an empire builder before he became city builder. The empire he built was the Shi'ite Fatimid, then based at Qayrawan. As commander in chief of the army, Jawhar achieved his first conquest in the Maghrib, where he extended (958) Fatimid domain to the Atlantic. As tangible evidence of his feat he sent to al-Mu'izz (953–975), fourth Fatimid caliph, live fish in huge water-filled jars. What makes the conquest more remarkable was the fact that the area was then contested by the mighty Spanish Umayyad caliph 'Abd-al-Rahman III. But Fatimid aspirations were oriented more eastward, toward

110

the heart of Islam and the seat of the political rival and religious enemy. Egypt lay between.

I

In 969 General Jawhar at the head of 100,000 strong launched his campaign with authority equal only to that of his caliph. Proper preparations had been made. Secret agents were dispatched to Egypt. Wells were dug along the desert route. Governors of provinces en route were ordered to receive the army chief ceremonially and kiss his hand. One of them offered 100,000 dinars to be spared the indignity of such homage to an ex-Christian slave, but to no avail. The valley of the Nile had been under a century of autonomous Turkish rule — Tulunid and Ikhshidid — and had extended its sway over Hijaz and part of Syria, but was ripe for conquest. Exploited by Turkish and Sudanese soldiery, ravaged by famine and plague, and softened by shrewd Fatimid propaganda, its leaderless people were in no position to resist. Alexandria submitted without a fight. The capital city, Fustat, was entered after an encounter in June at Jizah (Gizah), site of the great pyramids and the Sphinx. The new acquisition gave the rising Fatimid empire one of the richest if not the richest province of Islam. In comparison with Arabia and Syria, even with Iraq, the natural resources of the valley of the Nile seemed inexhaustible. The addition of Syria would make the rising empire contiguous to Iraq, and the addition of the Holy Cities of Hijaz would add inestimable prestige.

The victor lost no time in laying the foundation of his new capital. The site he chose excelled that of Baghdad in the number and importance of its forerunners, and the region around the site vied with that of the earlier capital. Here stood the Roman-Byzantine fortress Babylon, the Babalyun 'Amr ibn-al-'As captured in 641. The fortress reportedly owed its name to emigrants from Mesopotamia. The military camp 'Amr planted alongside the fortress grew into a city, Fustat, meaning "camp," "tent." The "tent town" was the first Arab foundation in Egypt. Its remains, as well as those of Babalyun, are included today in Misr al-'Atiqah (Old Cairo), mostly a Coptic quarter. The founder of the Tulunid dynasty set up northeast of Fustat a new establishment called Qata'i' (wards, quarters), designed to meet the needs of his residence and that of the different nationalities and classes in his entourage. The site Jawhar chose, then, had been chosen by three former builders. It lay northeast of Qata'i' and thirteen miles from the apex of the Delta.

The region saw the rise and fall of two ancient capitals, Memphis and Heliopolis, centuries before the Egyptian Babalyun was born. Traditionally the capital of Menes, first ruler of united Egypt, and historically the capital of his successors down to the twelfth dynasty (ca. 1786 B.C.), Memphis lay about fourteen miles south on the west bank of the river. The Saqqarah pyramids mark its site. The ruins of Heliopolis (On, 'Ayn Shams), religious capital of Lower Egypt, lie six miles northeast of modern Cairo. Dedicated to the worship of Ra, the sun deity, Memphis' temple served as a depository of historical and religious records. Obelisks from this city now decorate Rome, London's Thames Embankment, and New York's Central Park.

Such a site as that chosen by Jawhar must have had special geographic advantages. Lying near the point of the Delta's convergence toward the narrow valley of Upper Egypt, it was a meeting place of land and river routes and commanded the two parts of the country. Travelers from North Africa to western Asia found it easier to make the detour south than to go directly east through a marshy area. The existence of an islet, Rawdah, and the forking of the river facilitated the crossing. To its southwest lay the Fayyum oasis, the most fertile part of a fertile country. Specifically, the Fatimid general chose an alluvial plain at a point where the 550-foot-high Muqattam comes nearest to the river, providing a measure of protection against flood. A lot of about 1,200 yards square was marked by poles with ropes extending from one pole to the other. Mattocks in hand, laborers stood waiting for the sound of bells strung on the ropes, while astrologers were busy calculating the most favorable conjunction of the planets to give the signal for starting digging. But an impatient raven darted down, perched on the rope, and set the bells jingling. Down went the diggers' mattocks. Mars (Qahir al-Aflak, the subduer of the skies) was then at its zenith. The time (July 9, 969) was judged inauspicious. Babylonian stargazers had noted reddish orange glow on the surface of this planet (modern astronomers attribute the odd color to a deposit of iron-rock minerals) and regarded it as an omen of bloodshed and disaster. But al-Mu'izz, himself an authority on astrology, had a solution for the problem. By naming the new town al-Qahirah (whence

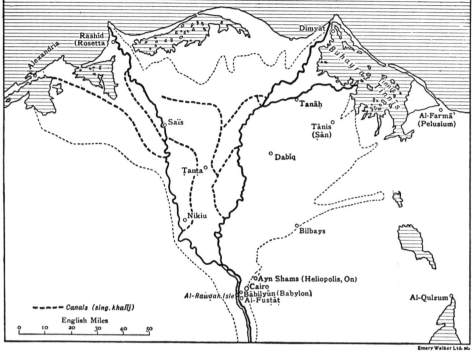

Early Egypt, illustrating the site and region of Cairo

Cairo, through Italian) the ominous sign was turned into an auspicious one. So auspicious it was as to make of it one of the world's cities of destiny.

"Al-Qahirah" — in full "Misr al-Qahirah" — remained the official title. The name by which it is commonly known is Misr (Masr), a relic of its ancient Semitic name. Whether there was a town in the neighborhood by that name is not certain. Before Cairo, Fustat was often compounded with Misr. The Hebrew name of the country is Misrayim, which in the biblical chronological table (Gen. 10:6) is used as the name of Ham's son. The Koran (10:87; 12:21, 100; 43:50) gives Egypt its right name, Misr.

Jawhar's first step after laying down the city wall with four gates was to start on the two major buildings: the caliphal palace and the mosque. The palace complex occupied the central area of 116,844 square yards. It was large enough to hold the imperial household and bodyguard and to provide offices for government officials and army officers. In course of time it came to have four thousand rooms. Close

113

by the palace rose the mosque extending to the foot of the Muqattam. It took two years (970–972) to build. Its name al-Azhar (the most resplendent) recalls 'Ali's wife and Muhammad's daughter, Fatimah al-Zahra'. Both palace and mosque assumed in course of time dimensions far beyond the fondest hopes of their Neo-Moslem builder, one becoming the richest royal residence in later Islam, and the other one of the most influential religious and educational centers of all time. In its thousand years of existence al-Azhar has defied attempts at radical reform, including wholesale modernization, and remained steadfast in its dedication to the study of the sacred law and the Arabic language. As for the city itself, it is today the most populous one in Africa. In July 1969 more than 4,000,000 people crowded into its 83 square miles to celebrate its thousandth anniversary.

It was time for the caliph in whose name the conquest was achieved to claim his prize. In June 973 al-Mu'izz entered his new palace in state. His baggage included a strange item: three coffins enclosing the remains of his predecessors. As he took his seat on the golden throne to receive the homage of his new subjects, Jawhar offered his in the form of a present comprising, among other valuable items, 150 horses (some with jeweled saddles), 9 camels loaded with silk cloth, and 4 boxes filled with gold and silver vases. The general was confirmed in the governorship of the country. The 'Abbasid caliph's name had already been expunged from all official records and the Friday prayer. A new coinage was struck. In place of black, the official 'Abbasid color, white was ordained. On the day of al-Azhar's dedication the preacher invoked Allah's blessings on the "Imam al-Mu'izz li-Din Allah [the strengthener of the religion of Allah], the commander of the believers" and on his ancestors of the holy family going back to 'Ali. A new era dawned on the valley of the Nile, indeed on Africa. For the first time in a thousand years Egypt could claim it was again a fully sovereign state. The Fatimid caliph was more than a caliph; he was an imam, a spiritual leader with a charisma stemming from 'Ali and Muhammad through Fatimah. Unlike the Sunni caliph he was a kind of a pope ruling with divine right.

Al-Mu'izz' great-grandfather, the founder of the dynasty, took the name of 'Ubaydullah al-Mahdi (909–934) and claimed descent from Fatimah through the seventh Imam Isma'il (d. 760). One of the most

The Azhar Mosque in Cairo

enigmatic personages in Moslem history, 'Ubaydullah assumed a name meaning the "small slave of Allah" but behaved as if he was himself divine. His opponents maintained that he was an impostor named Sa'id, descended from a Persian occultist. His birthplace Salamyah was and still is an Isma'ili center in northern Syria. Sunni historians deny Fatimids the right to so call themselves and prefer to call them 'Ubaydids. The Isma'ili headquarters in Persia was Alamut west of Teheran near the Caspian Sea, where they became known as Assassins. The followers of Isma'il were also called Seveners in opposition to the Twelvers, who formed the bulk of the Shi'ite body. In 909 'Ubaydullah destroyed the century-old Sunni Aghlabid dynasty of Qayrawan and fell heir to a large part of North Africa, Sicily, and a well-equipped fleet.

115

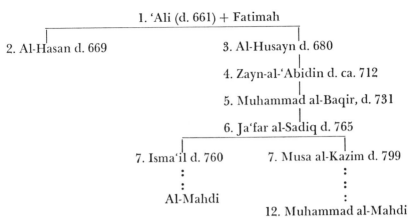

1. 'Ali (d. 661) + Fatimah

2. Al-Hasan d. 669   3. Al-Husayn d. 680

4. Zayn-al-'Abidin d. ca. 712

5. Muhammad al-Baqir, d. 731

6. Ja'far al-Sadiq d. 765

7. Isma'il d. 760   7. Musa al-Kazim d. 799

⋮   ⋮

Al-Mahdi   ⋮

12. Muhammad al-Mahdi

The Relationship of the Seven and Twelf Shi'ite Imams

'Ubaydullah's triumph was the culmination of two and a half centuries of 'Alid struggle, beginning with 'Ali's death, to gain the headship of Islam. Throughout the period 'Alids never ceased to plot and conspire — under and above ground; to riot and fight; to invoke Allah's blessings on their imams and curses on the usurpers — but all in vain. Their goal behaved as elusively as the mirage of the Arabian desert. The Umayyad and 'Abbasid authorities spared no Shi'ite pretender. Four of the ten imams descended from the "martyred" son of 'Ali, al-Husayn, were certainly or suspiciously poisoned by secret agents from Baghdad.

II

The installation of al-Mu'izz in the new capital involved more than a change in geography and religion. It involved changes in the political, social, and cultural traditions of the country and raised Egypt to a leading position in the world of Islam — a position it held into the Ottoman conquest five and a half centuries later.

The first order of business before the new administration was to restore order to a chaotic land and to ensure its hold upon its two outlying provinces. The situation in Syria, to which Jawhar before this had sent his lieutenant, necessitated the use of the sword, but that of Hijaz required the use of gold. Next to internal security the domestic situation required reform of the financial system and improvement of the economy. To this end lands illegally sequestered by former regimes were returned to their rightful owners, and vexatious taxes were abolished. Monopolists of grain and profiteers of black market were fought. A public depot of wheat was established under government auspices. A converted Jew, Ya'qub ibn-Killis, was the caliph's right hand in these reforms. Of Baghdadi origin, Ya'qub had labored in Egypt and had played a role in encouraging the country's invasion by correspondence with al-Mu'izz.

On the sectarian side, the caliph exercised commendable restraint, despite the reputed intolerance of Isma'ilism. Realizing that the country was predominantly Sunni, he took no extreme measures for conversion. He, however, took pains to make of the Azhar, a center of Shi'ite propaganda. Of al-Mu'izz' policy of religious tolerance, native Christians were the chief beneficiary. He had lived in Sicily and acquired foreign languages. As the Copts prospered they rebuilt ruined churches and took a step upward in the social ladder. Meantime the fleet, an important source of strength and income, was not neglected. Docks were built along the Nile, hundreds of ships were added — some measuring 275 by 110 feet — and sea trade with Europe was conducted on a larger scale than before. The Egyptian income rose to a figure approaching the maximum of four million dinars under the Umayyads.

The new prosperity was reflected in the caliphal life. Al-Mu'izz enlarged and embellished the palace and indulged in luxury. He thereby set the sumptuous tone which was to characterize the following period. For a silk Persian rug depicting the countries of the world, he reportedly paid 35,000 dinars. One of his daughters is said to have left her heirs no less than 2,700,000 dinars, and another daughter 3,000 silver vessels, 5 sacks of emerald, Sicilian embroideries, and other valuables requiring forty pounds of wax to seal.

The new capital on the Nile enjoyed three periods of glory: one under the Fatimids, another under the Ayyubid Salah-al-Din, and a third under the Mamluk sultans Baybars and al-Nasir. The Fatimid period began with al-Mu'izz and reached its climax under his son al-'Aziz (975–996).

Al-'Aziz followed in his father's three-pronged policy of reform in administration, economic development, and religious tolerance. The twenty-year-old caliph was fortunate in having inherited from his

117

father both Jawhar and ibn-Killis, on whom he bestowed for the first time in Fatimid history the title of vizir. Among the new fiscal reforms were assigning fixed salaries for troops, palace personnel, and other government officials. Ibn-Killis' pay reached 100,000 dinars annually. The new system was meant to deter bribe. The caliph launched a new program of building mosques, palaces, and bridges as well as digging new canals. He had another vizir, a Christian as indicated by the name 'Isa ibn-Nasturus, who built a navy that contributed to security and prosperity. Fatimid estrangement from the bulk of the Moslem community in the East made the authorities turn for fresh sources of income from the West.

With the new wave of prosperity, al-'Aziz was able to indulge his lavish tastes. These included fondness for strange animals, especially birds — which he imported from Sudan — and sea fish. This, however, did not inhibit his interest in hunting lions. He was also a connoisseur of jewelry and art and was credited with two fashionable creations: gold-thread turbans and jeweled harnesses scented with ambergis. Once his pigeon carriers treated him to cherries from Baalbak. His generosity went beyond himself. He surrounded himself with theologians, scholars, and men of letters and assigned them pensions — of course, expecting their sympathy and support by way of reward. The caliph was himself an amateur scholar; he composed poetry, wrote and copied books, and established a library in the palace. He endowed al-Azhar — hitherto a religious propaganda center — and converted it into a teaching institute of the university type — a position that it holds to the present.

Fatimid tolerance had no doubt a political aspect. Being alienated from their Sunni subjects, the successors of 'Ubaydullah felt a loyalty gap and hesitated to appoint their subjects to the highest office. In the case of al-'Aziz there was in addition a personal reason: the influence of his Christian Russian wife. Her son al-Hakim he designated for successor. The lady had two brothers, one of whom was made Melkite patriarch of Egypt and the other of Jerusalem. The Coptic patriarch was also befriended and allowed to rebuild a church he could not build before. That al-'Aziz was by nature both humane and wise is best illustrated by his treatment of a Turk from Baghdad, Aftakin, who installed himself as an 'Abbasid agent in Damascus. After Jawhar had led an unsuccessful campaign against the rebel, the caliph moved in person against him and having defeated him, pressed him, together with his Turkish troops, into his service and bestowed special honors on him. Hitherto Berber troops were the main support of the dynasty. The introduction of Turkish mercenaries into Cairo was almost as fateful a step as their introduction into Baghdad.

Under the reign of the first caliph to commence his rule in Egypt, Cairo had become not only a formidable rival of Baghdad but its superior. Its state had become the leading Moslem state in the eastern Mediterranean. So sure was al-'Aziz of his final victory that he erected a two-million-dinar palace in his capital to house his 'Abbasid rival on capturing him. Before his death at the age of forty-one his name was cited in the Friday sermons from the Atlantic to the Red Sea, from southern Yaman to northern Syria, and at least once in northern Iraq (Mosul).

Al-Hakim (996–1021), an unworthy successor of a worthy father, came to the throne at the age of eleven. His official title was al-Kakim bi-Amr-Allah (he who rules by the order of Allah) but he began early on attaining age to rule by his own orders. Not only did he reactivate discriminatory regulations against Dhimmis initiated by the Umayyad caliph 'Umar II and the 'Abbasid al-Mutawakkil but he added stringent ones. In a series of decrees between 1004 and 1013 this son of a Christian mother forced Christians and Jews to wear distinctive black belts and turbans and when in the public baths to hang crosses and bells respectively round their necks. They could ride only on donkeys. The use of wine was prohibited even in churches. All public religious processions were forbidden, and so was the display of crosses. A number of monasteries and churches in Egypt, Syria, and Palestine, including the Holy Sepulcher, were demolished. Christian government officials were executed, not sparing the vizir 'Isa ibn-Nasturus. With equal illogic al-Hakim refused to enforce the law of apostasy, involving death, on those Christians who to escape persecution temporarily embraced Islam — his theologians' insistence notwithstanding.

If any of his Moslem subjects had resented the traditional treatment of non-Moslems and felt gratified by the new anti-Christian measures, they were soon to learn that excesses knew no religious boundaries. Moslem vizirs and officials were among the victims. For a riot in Fustat he ordered fire set, leaving a quarter in ruins. The reasons for the executions varied and so did the methods. Drowning was favored for his concubines. Women in general were forbidden to adorn themselves, display jewelry, or appear in public baths or at cemeteries and, by way of implementation, shoemakers were ordered not to make shoes for them. One of the leading physicists of the age, ibn-al-Haytham (Lat. Alhazen, d. 1030) simulated madness to escape the caliph's rage aroused by the scholar's failure to regulate the annual flow of the Nile. It was ibn-al-Haytham who in his work on optics corrected Euclid's theory that the eyes send out visual rays to the object of vision.

One bright spot there was in the dark record of this Fatimid. In 1005 he, inspired by al-Ma'mun's precedent, erected a "hall of science and wisdom," endowed it with funds and stocked it with books, making it a center for teaching astronomy and medicine, additional to Islamic subjects with stress on their Shi'ite aspect.

In 1017 al-Hakim crowned his strange career by proclaiming himself the incarnation of the deity — a step he took under encouragement from extremists in Isma'ilism. His missionaries spread the new cult in and outside of Egypt, but it took permanent root only in southern Lebanon, whence it passed to Syria. In both countries its adherents are known as Druzes after its propagandist al-Darazi. The cult made al-Hakim's name the best known in the Fatimid series.

On a dark February night in 1021, as al-Hakim was having his usual walk on the Muqattam, he ordered his two attendants to await his return, and moved on — never to return. One explanation for his disappearance is that his sister, resenting his excesses and charged by him with inchastity, had masterminded his secret murder. His followers, however, interpreted his disappearance as a voluntary and temporary episode in the career of a divine being.

III

Although riots and rebellions in Egypt, North Africa, and Syria were rife during al-Hakim's reign, the realm was passed virtually intact to his sixteen-year-old son al-Zahir (1021–1036). But the writing on the wall was unmistakable. The Cairo dynasty was inscribing the life cycle marked by the Damascus and the Baghdad dynasties: a beginning under vigorous, aggressive founder or founders, attainment of a peak with a plateau for a couple of regimes, and then down a precipitous path to disintegration. The disintegrating forces in this case included, on the political side, immature, incompetent, and disinterested caliphs surrounded by vizirs struggling for power and depending on the favors of competing army generals of Berber, Turkish, and Sudanese battalions. All eight successors of al-Hakim came to the throne before attaining maturity. His son al-Mustansir was eleven. The last in the series, al-'Adid (number 14, d. 1171) was nine. That in itself constituted an invitation to vizirs to usurp the supreme power. It made of the Cairo caliphs no less puppets in the hands of vizirs and generals than the Baghdad caliphs had been.

Al-Zahir began his career under the tutelage of his maternal aunt. Riots continued in his reign spreading into Hijaz, where an Egyptian pilgrim tried to destroy the Black Stone. Al-Mustansir began under the regency of his mother, once a slave from Sudan purchased from a Jew who now shared authority with her. Then al-Mustansir had an Armenian vizir, also an ex-slave, named Badr al-Jamali. Badr bequeathed the office to his son under the title al-Malik al-Afdal (the superior monarch). An unusually able administrator, Badr tried hard but could not check the downward trend. A later vizir was a Kurd. Clearly this Shi'ite caliphate was no more able to integrate Berbers and Sudanese than the Sunnite caliphate had been able to integrate Persians and Turks. More than that, the Shi'i-Sunni gap in the Fatimid state remained open and deep. Hard as they tried to ingratiate themselves with their Moslem subjects by patronizing art and building mosques, schools, and other public works, the alienation continued.

Other than for its length, the reign of al-Mustansir (1035–1094), the longest in Moslem annals, was distinguished by the loss of Syria, North Africa, and Hijaz. The mention of al-Mustansir's name in the Baghdad mosques' prayers by a Shi'ite rebel al-Basasiri (960), who also sent to Cairo the 'Abbasid caliph's turban, mantle, and other emblems and sacred relics, made no difference. The weakness of the central government encouraged separatist movements in the provinces. By 1076 Syria had become a Saljuq domain owing allegiance to Baghdad. Berber states mushroomed to the west of Egypt. Mecca discontinued the sermons in the Fatimid name when the subsidy was discontinued.

The political disruptive forces were compounded by economic ones. As the empire shrank its revenue decreased. International trade dwindled. Neglect of canals and misbehavior on the part of the inundating Nile precipitated famines, one of which under al-Mustansir lasted seven years. With famine went plague. All the while caliphs continued to indulge their tastes for luxury and the vizirs their insatiable greed, resulting in extortions and overtaxation. Al-Mustansir, who inherited millions from his predecessors, excelled them all in loose living and ostentation. He created for himself a Kaabah-like pavilion dedicated to music and song. To him, in his own words, "That was more pleasurable than staring at a Black Stone, listening to the muezzin's drone and drinking impure water." An Egyptian historian, al-Maqrizi, left us an elaborate inventory of the caliphal treasures. Listed among other items were precious stones, crystal vases, inlaid gold plates, ivory inkstands, amber cups, phials of musk, steel mirrors, jeweled daggers and swords, and embroidered fabrics, manufactured in Egypt and Syria. In 1047 the learned Persian traveler Nasir-i-Khusrau visited Cairo, saw the caliph and his palace, and in glowing terms described what he saw:

Cairo is a great city to which few cities can be compared. I estimated no fewer than 20,000 shops in Cairo owned by the sultan. A large number of them rent for 10 Maghribi dinars per month; only a few rent for less than 2 dinars.

Caravanseries, baths and other public structures are so numerous as to be difficult to count — all the property of the sultan, for no one could possess a house or a building unless the one he himself built. In each of Cairo, I was told, and of Misr [Fustat] as many as 20,000 houses belong to the sultan.[1]

The caliphal palace, the narrator goes on to say, housed 30,000 persons of whom 12,000 were servants and 1,000 horse and foot guards. Al-Mustansir looked pleasant and clean shaven at a festival as he rode on a mule. An attendant held over his head a parasol enriched with precious stones. The whole country looked so prosperous to this Isma'ili visitor that he enthusiastically declared that nowhere had he seen comparable wealth. Certain houses, mostly of brick, rose to a height of seven stories; one of them had on top a terrace garden of orange and other fruit trees. Cairo had eight great mosques; Fustat had eight. The main streets were roofed and lighted by lamps. On December 18, 1048, Nasir found in the markets red roses, lilies, sweet and bitter oranges, lemons, apples, grapes, dates, sugar canes, gourds,

1. Nasir-i Khosrau, *Sefar, Nameh*, ed. and tr. Charles Schefer (Paris, 1881), p. 127.

onions, garlic, carrots and other fruits, flowers, and vegetables. The bazars had huge copper bowls made in Damascus, pottery so fine that one could see his hand through it, and rich cloth made in Egypt and Syria. Prices — strange as it may seem — were fixed. If a shopkeeper cheated, he would be paraded on a camel through the streets shouting to the ringing of a bell: "I have cheated and am punished. May the like punishment befall all liars!"

Yet, difficult as it may be to believe, barely twenty-two years after this description, al-Mustansir found himself in such destitution that he had to sell his treasures and send his mother and daughters to Baghdad to escape starvation.

IV

Three years after the death of al-Mustansir, the world of Islam was unexpectedly treated to a strange phenomenon: hordes of Europeans, wearing the cross as a badge, pouring into the Saljuq domain of Asia Minor. Their avowed purpose: to wrest the Holy Land from "infidels' " hands. The march through Syria, after the occupation of Antioch in 1098, was more of a promenade. In the following year Jerusalem was conquered and its inhabitants were subjected to an indiscriminate slaughter. Antioch was under Saljugs, Jerusalem under Fatamids. Damascus was bypassed. It was inland and difficult to defend. Jerusalem became the capital of a Latin kingdom, which by 1118 extended from Beirut to the Red Sea. The newly established principalities of Antioch and Tripoli were attached to it by feudal bonds. It soon became apparent that the acquisition of Egypt, because of its geographic position and economic prosperity, was essential for the safety of the new state.

In 1168 King Amalric of Jerusalem, realizing the decrepit condition of Egypt, entered into secret negotiations with a displaced perfidious vizir, named Shawar, and moved intent upon its conquest. He had made an earlier attempt. Caliph al-'Adid (1160–1171) had only one available source of support: Damascus. The city was then under the rule of a Turk, Nur-al-Din, whose father Zangi of Mosul had extended his domain as far as Aleppo. Nur sent an expeditionary force under General Shirkuh assisted by a twenty-nine–year–old nephew Salah-al-Din. Born in Iraq, Salah was brought up first in Damascus and then in Baalbak, where his father served as governor. As Amalric approached the capital, al-'Adid considered it expedient to set its Fustat quarter on fire. Some 20,000 barrels of naphtha, we are told, and 10,000 lighted lamps made of the old city for 54 days a bonfire whose traces can still be found in the sandheaps stretching for miles south of modern Cairo. The clouds of smoke kept the enemy away. Early in January 1169 the Damascene general who came as a deliverer, as often happens, remained as a conqueror. Shirkuh seized the vizirate for himself and bequeathed it two months later to his nephew. In a pantomine ceremony the Fatimid caliph bestowed on Salah-al-Din (rectitude of faith, Saladin), an officer in the army of a Sunni monarch of Damascus, the vizirial robe and with it the title of al-Malik al-Nasir (the supporter-king).

The new vizir was quick to act. He brought his family to Cairo, organized his own army of Syrians, Kurds, and loyal Egyptians, appointed his two brothers as commanders, and put the caliph's palace under a new guard. When two years later al-'Adid lay on his deathbed the preacher in the congregational mosque was heard for the first time in two centuries imploring Allah to preserve His servant and the son of His servant the 'Abbasid caliph. So smooth was the transition that in the words of a chronicler "there was not so much as the butting of two goats."

A contemporary Arab historian, ibn-al-Athir, described the treasures found in the caliphal palace by Salah-al-Din:

So numerous were the treasures that they could not be counted. Among them were precious pendants and other strange jewelry the like of which can be found nowhere. There were also gems unique in kind and size. One mountain-size ruby was seventeen dirhams or miskals [2,400 carats]. There can be no doubt about it; I saw it with my eyes and weighed it myself. The pearls also had no peer. Among the emeralds was one four fingers long.[2]

The disposition Salah made of the inherited treasures stands out as an exceptional procedure in Arab annals. After sending his sovereign Nur in Damascus his share and distributing a part among his officers, he sold the rest for the state treasury, leaving nothing for himself. A large part of the caliphal library of 120,000 manuscripts he bestowed

2. Ibn-al-Athir, *Kamil al-Tawarikh*, ed. C. J. Tornberg, vol. XI (Uppsala, 1851), p. 242.

on his secretary and trusted counselor al-Qadi al-Fadil. As for the royal palace he spurned it in favor of the vizirial mansion in keeping with his style of life, which could be characterized as ascetic in contrast to that of his uncle, who two months after assuming power died of over-eating.

The Fatimid dynasty passed into the limbo of history, but Fatimid relics in art and architecture remained for the viewer to enjoy and for the student to investigate. Of the mosques the oldest, al-Azhar — renovated more than once — is the most conspicuous. Three massive gates of the city are extant and promise to endure. Fatimid architects followed in the Moslem tradition but introduced novel features, such as stalactite pendentives and deep niches in the façades that were developed under the succeeding Ayyubid and Mamluk dynasties.

In decorative and industrial arts, likewise Fatimid craftsmen borrowed mainly from Sasanid models, but introduced new elements. Fatimids were dissidents in more than religion. Specimens in museums display living animals, bronze mirrors, ewers and incensers, ceramic and metallic pieces, glazed earthenware. These, together with rich cloth and carved wood panels, corroborate al-Maqrizi's and Nasir-i-Khusrau's reports. In the textile industry two Egyptian cities gave their names to their products. The fustian cloth known to Chaucer was made in Fustat. The *tinnisi* cloth, from which presumably the first tennis balls were made, giving its name to the game, was manufactured in Tinnis, a city in the Delta.

V

Salah-al-Din terminated Cairo's career as a dissident capital, but started it on a new career as an orthodox one. As sultan he ruled independently, owing nominal political allegiance to Damascus and religious allegiance to Baghdad. The city maintained its position as capital throughout the rule of the Ayyubid dynasty (so-called after Salah's father Ayyub, Job) and its successor the Mamluk dynasty — a period of two and a half centuries.

By destroying the Fatimid regime Salah realized the first of a triple ambition of his life. The remaining two involved uniting Egypt and

Syria under one scepter and then putting the Latin Kingdom of Jerusalem under an upper and a lower millstone and crushing it. The death of Nur-al-Din in 1174 gave him the chance to attain the second goal. The succession of Nur's eleven-year-old son to the Syrian throne and the struggle for power by viziers and army officers ended on October 24 when the sultan of Egypt, at the head of seven hundred picked horsemen, entered the Syrian capital unopposed. The dash was made through the desert and escaped the vigilance of Crusading garrisons along the eastern border of Palestine. Cairo was left in charge of one of his brothers. Damascene officials, theologians, and laymen hastened to offer homage to the new champion of Islam and worthy heir of Nur and Zangi. In the meantime the child-king had been moved to Aleppo, whose eunuch governor had thrown his rivals for the vice-regency into jail and abrogated the high office for himself. Salah married Nur's widow, a familiar practice under such circumstances, and proceeded north to consolidate his control over Syria, leaving his brother Sayf-al-Islam (the sword of Islam) in charge. On the battlefield outside Hamah, Salah met a combination of forces from Aleppo, Mosul, and other royalist towns and routed them. The victory sealed the fate of Syria as far as the upper reaches of the Tigris. Hijaz, Yaman, and Cyrenaica had already been annexed.

Back in Cairo the sultan of Egypt-Syria was now in a position to seek the ultimate goal of his life. To him as to his coreligionists Jerusalem (Bayt al-Maqdis, colloquially al-Quds, the house of holiness) was the third holiest city. It was the first kiblah (*qiblah,* direction to which Moslems turn in praying) of Islam, the stopping place of the Prophet on his nocturnal journey heavenward, and the promised meeting place on the last day. Its wresting from Christian hands would be the crowning achievement of his entire career.

Cautiously he proceeded to measure swords with the enemy. Leading 27,000 men he entered southern Palestine on November 10, 1177, captured Ascalon ('Asqalan), plundered its region, and proceeded along the coast bypassing Jerusalem. The first serious encounter took place at Ramlah. There the Franks (to use the term — Faranj — the natives gave to all Europeans) had assembled contingents from Jerusalem, Sidon, and Karak (Crac des Moabites), a mighty fortress on the caravan route at the southern extremity of the Dead Sea. The host featured the Knights of the Temple, so named because the order was founded (1118) in the Temple of Solomon to protect pilgrims and fight with other Crusaders. In the course of the combat Salah was somehow isolated from his troops, his bodyguard was almost anni-hilated, and he himself had a narrow escape under night cover on a swift dromedary.

The experience was humiliating but not disheartening. Two years later, with fresh recruits from Damascus, Salah was ready for a new round. King Baldwin, son and successor of Amalric, was then building a fort at a passage over the Jordan named Jacob's Ford (Banat Ya'qub), the traditional site of Jacob's wrestling with the angel. Because of its strategic importance as opening the way to Damascus and more im-mediately to the fertile plain of Baniyas (Banias), the sultan offered the king a price of 10,000 gold pieces, but Baldwin would not desist. Baldwin was afflicted with leprosy and lacked the ability of his father. The fort was protected by a thirteen-foot-wide wall of solid masonry and defended by the flower of the Crusading military organization — the Templars. The attempt on it began on August 25, 1179. After days of valiant resistance the besiegers effected a breach in the wall, stormed the fort, put its garrison to the sword, and took seven hundred pris-oners. The victorious commander withstood the corpses' stench in the summer sun until the last vestige of the structures had been disman-tled. A two-year-truce was signed.

The long-deferred showdown at last came. The day was June 26, 1189. Salah at the head of 12,000 horsemen and 6,000 footmen, mus-tered from Cairo, Damascus, Aleppo, and Mosul, marched against Tiberias. In six days the city surrendered. Meantime King Guy of Jerusalem had amassed 4,700 knights and horsemen and 18,000 foot-men, from Jerusalem, Karak, Tripoli, and other dependencies. Ray-mond, count of Tripoli, was there in person; so was Reginald, French lord of Karak. In addition to the Templars, Hospitalers were there. Also called the Knights of St. John of Jerusalem, the order of Hospital-ers was originally instituted to provide hostel service to pilgrims. On Friday July 3, the two camps stood facing each other on an uneven plateau named Hittin overlooking the Lake of Galilee. In the follow-ing two days, the Crusading host, with heavily armed men, thirsty and exhausted by the long march, were mercilessly cut down. Before the battle cry of "Allahu akbar," the cross held high by the bishop of Acre seemed helpless. The rout was complete. The few who sought escape in flight or apostasy were lucky. Less lucky were the prisoners headed by Guy and Reginald. Raymond had fled. For Templars and Hospitalers, personifying the military ego of the Crusaders, there was no amnesty. The king was assured by the sultan that he would be treated in a way worthy of his status. As for the treacherous Reginald, who not only had repeatedly intercepted and pillaged merchants' and pilgrims' caravans passing by his castle but ventured to launch a project in Hijaz aiming at seizing the Prophet's body and exhibiting it for a fee, there was no mercy. Salah had vowed to slaughter him with his own hand. He never violated a pledge. But King Guy, who had been freed from captivity on his word of honor never to bear arms again, was in two years fighting again at Acre against his benefactor.

The victory of Hittin marked the beginning of the end of Crusading dominance in the Holy Land. Defenseless Jerusalem surrendered. Its fall aroused Christendom. Three crowned heads, Philip Augustus of France, Frederick Barbarossa of Germany, and Richard the Lion-Hearted of England, were soon on the war path. The aged Frederick was drowned en route in Asia Minor. Philip hastened back home after a short and ineffective stay. The small town of Acre ('Akka), on a tongue of land jutting out southward into the sea, provided the scene for the two champions of the East and the West to perform their feats of valor, commemorated in legend and history. After two years of siege (1189–1191) the city fell into Richard's hands. A peace was concluded stipulating that the coast from Tyre south be given to the Latins, while the hinterland — including Jerusalem — would be left in Moslem hands. Two years later the fifty-four-year old sultan died of fever in his Syrian capital and was buried outside of its great mosque, where his shrine still stands as an object of visitation.

To the legacy of shining chivalry and staunch championship of orthodoxy, the hero of Islam added patronage of learning. Though by his time the sources of creative scholarship in Islam had practically dried, Salah erected academic institutions, mostly of the collegiate-mosque type combining theological seminaries, law academies, and schools of

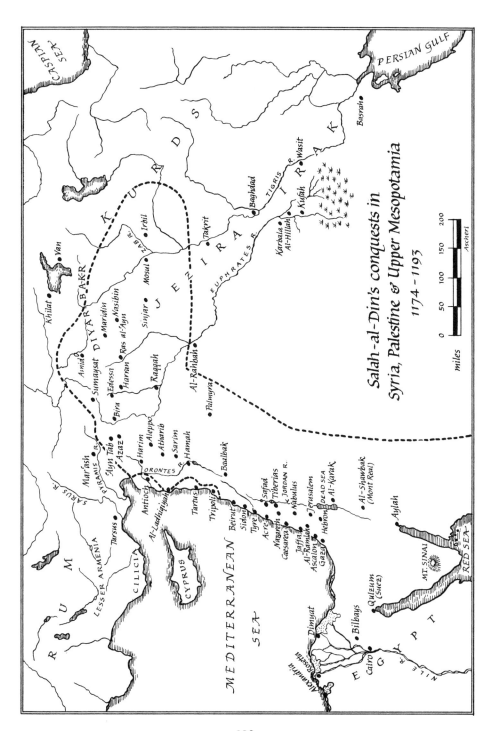

Salah-al-Din's conquests in
Syria, Palestine & Upper Mesopotamia
1174–1193

CASPIAN SEA

PERSIAN GULF

Basrah

Baghdad

Wasit

Kufah

Karbala
Al-Hillah

Takrit

Irbil

Mosul

Sinjar

Nasibin

Maridin

Ras al-'Ayn

Harran

Raqqah

Al-Rahbah

Palmyra

Van

Khilat

Amid

Sumaysat

Edessa

Bira

Mar'ash

'Ayn Tab

Azaz

Harim

Aleppo

Atharib

Sarim

Hamah

Baalbak

Al-Shawbak
(Mont Real)

Aylah

Antioch

Al-Laahiqiyah

Tartus

Tripoli

Beirut

Sidon

Tyre

Acre

Nazareth

Caesarea

Jaffa

Al-Ramlah

Ascalon

Gaza

Safad

Tiberias

Nabulus

Jerusalem

Hebron

Al-Karak

DEAD SEA

JORDAN R.

Tarsus

CILICIA

LESSER ARMENIA

CYPRUS

MEDITERRANEAN SEA

Dimyat

Alexandria

Rosetta

Cairo

Bilbays

Qulzum
(Suez)

MT. SINAI

RED SEA

EGYPT

NILE R.

KURDS

DIYAR BAKR

JEZIRA

IRAQ

RUM

ORONTES

EUPHRATES R.

TIGRIS R.

ZABR.

SARUS R.

PYRAMIS R.

miles

0   50   100   150   200

Ascherl

129

letters, all supported by the state. The literary products of his and his successors' age featured biographical dictionaries, historical compendiums, legal manuals, and theological commentaries. Medicine was taught in hospitals on which the sultan bestowed his special care. Ibn-Jubayr visited (1183) and admiringly described the Cairo hospital.

Another object we witnessed in Cairo in which the sultan can take justifiable pride was the hospital (*maristan*) for the insane. The building is truly palatial in spaciousness and magnificence. This beneficent deed was undertaken by the sultan in quest of heavenly reward. The hospital was put in charge of a knowledgeable director and provided with drugs in cupboards and a variety of medicinal drinks to be administered by him. The bedrooms were fully equipped for the patients' use. The director had under him attendants responsible for visiting patients morning and evening, and administering whatever food and medicine were required.

Facing this building was another structure reserved for women. Women also had responsible attendants. Adjoining the two buildings was a third one, large in size, with rooms provided with iron-latticed windows designed for the confinement of certain insane persons. These patients, too, had special attendants waiting on them to provide them with whatever was necessary.

The sultan in person oversees the entire institution, investigating, questioning and making sure that proper care is persistently given. Misr [Fustat] has a similar institution.[3]

Besides building schools, mosques, hospitals, and dervish monasteries, Salah repaired the old city walls and crowned its Muqattam with a citadel still dominating the entire scene. Next to Jawhar he stands out as a builder of Cairo. The citadel was separated from the Muqattam by a deep ditch and followed in its construction the fashion of the Crusading castle. It was used as a residence by him and his successors till after the days of Muhammad 'Ali (d. 1849), who added to it a conspicuous mosque.

The Syro-Egyptian realm left by Salah was fragmented among his sons and brothers and further weakened by their squabbles and internecine wars. When in 1249 the last Ayyubid died in Cairo, his widow Shajar-al-Durr (tree of pearl), originally a non-Arab slave, assumed control. The following year she married an army officer named Aybak, originally a Turkish slave in the last Ayyubid sultan's bodyguard.

3. Ibn-Jubayr, p. 26; cf. Broadhurst, pp. 43–44.

Muhammad 'Ali's mosque at Salah-al-Din's citadel

VI

Aybak (1250–1257) initiated a new line of Syro-Egyptian sultans, styled Mamluks (*mamluk*, non-black slave), which lasted until the conquest of the Ottoman Turks in 1517. Mostly Turks and Circassians, the Mamluk sultans were generally uncultured, bloodthirsty Neo-Moslems.

The most distinguished of the forty-seven Mamluks was unquestionably al-Zahir Baybars (1260–1277), another ex-slave of the last Ayyubid sultan. His former master had bought him from a Damascus market for eight hundred dirhams but returned him on discovering a defect in one of his blue eyes. With determination and energy worthy of a successor of Salah-al-Din, Baybars conducted nine campaigns against the Mongols who, after the destruction of Baghdad, had swept over Syria and Palestine, and many other campaigns against rebels and Isma'ilis in Syria and elsewhere. But the Crusaders were his enemy number one. Under his blows one after the other of the Crusaders' cities and strongholds — Caesarea, Arsuf, Jaffa — fell. In 1268 Antioch, after Jerusalem the most important town in Frankish hands, capitulated. Of its inhabitants and garrison 16,000 were slaughtered and

100,000 captured. Three years later Hisn al-Akrad (Crac des Chevaliers), tenaciously held by Hospitalers, yielded. In 1289 Tripoli surrendered and was left in ruins. Baybars' successors wrote *finis* on the two-century-old Moslem-Christian drama.

Under Baybars and his successors Cairo became the most distinguished center of Islam. This sultan repaired the city walls, renovated the Azhar, and in 1261 invited a scion of the 'Abbasid family, then a refugee in Damascus, to come to the capital where, in a pompous ceremony, he was installed as caliph. This gave legitimacy to the regime and enhanced its prestige particularly in Mecca and Medina. The sultan made an abortive attempt to reestablish the pseudo-caliph in Baghdad.

As an alien oligarchy in a land in whose soil they had no roots, the Mamluks, we learned, sought in public works a means of ingratiating themselves with their subjects. Hence the architectural and artistic activity on a scale and of a quality that had no equal in Egyptian Moslem history. Their school of architecture followed in the Nurid and Ayyubid tradition but received fresh influences as Cairo became a haven for Syro-Mesopotamian artists and artisans fleeing in the wake of Mongol invasions. The Mamluk monuments of Cairo stand out as the last ones of their kind in an Arab land.

In the unusually long three-period reign of the ninth Mamluk, al-Nasir (1293–1294, 1298–1308, 1309–1340), the sultanate may be said to have enjoyed its heyday of peace and prosperity. The sultan's extravagance and ostentation, on both personal and public levels, knew no bounds. The unique multicolored palace (al-Ablaq) he built for his residence became the talk of the town. Investing 30,000 dinars in a house he fancied was considered by him worthwhile. At his son's wedding 20,000 animals were slaughtered, 18,000 sugar loaves consumed, and 3,000 candles lighted. While on the holy pilgrimage the sultan had a garden on 40 camels to supply him with fresh vegetables throughout the desert journey. His public works covering the realm included 30 mosques and numberless dervish monasteries, drinking fountains, baths, and schools, one of which named after him al-Nasiriyah is still standing. His most ambitious project perhaps was linking Alexandria with the Nile by a canal on which 100,000 men toiled for long.

The famed Moroccan world-traveler ibn-Battutah visited al-Nasir's capital and described it in these glowing terms:

Then I arrived at Misr, mother of the country, ex-seat of Pharoah the tyrant, mistress of extensive provinces and fruitful territories, boundless in the number of buildings, peerless in beauty and splendor; the rendezvous of comers and goers and the stopping place of the powerful and the powerless. Therein you find as many as you want of the learned and the ignorant, the grave and the gay; the prudent and the insolent, the base and the noble, the honorable and the debased, the known and the unknown. As the sea surges with its waves, so does the city surge with its inhabitants whom it can hardly contain despite its spaciousness and capacity. Its youthfulness is ever young despite old age, and its horoscope star does not move from the mansion of fortune. Being al-Qahirah it has subdued nations and its kings have ruled over Arabs and non-Arabs.[4]

The long rhetoric is followed by short statistics. A fleet of 12,000 cameleers and 30,000 muleteers supply the city with drinking water, and 36,000 vessels, owned by the sultan and his people, ply from its Nile.

There was another side to the picture, however. The public works of al-Nasir and other Mamluks were largely carried out by forced labor and entailed mounting taxation. Famine and plague, endemic in Egypt, added their quota of misery, as they did under the Fatimids. The so-called black death, which in the mid-fourteenth century devastated Europe, originated in Egypt, where it raged for seven years, leaving — in the estimate of a chronicler flourishing in the following century — 900,000 victims, a number difficult to accept unless it be taken to mean for the whole country. It is equally difficult to believe an Italian traveler who visited Cairo in 1384, three years after the second plague, and found 100,000 sleeping outside doors in Cairo because of housing shortage.

The trouble was compounded by corruption, ruthlessness, negligence, and incompetence in high places. Hardly any of al-Nasir's successors achieved distinction in any field of endeavor. Some were degenerate. One beheaded two physicians for failure to cure the tyrant from a disease. Another was so illiterate that he could not sign his name except by tracing it over his secretary's writing, and could not recite the first surah of the Koran, repeated in the daily prayers, with-

4. Defrémery and Sanguinetti, Arabic text, vol. I, pp. 67–68; cf. Gibb, vol. I, p. 41.

out making a mistake. In fact, of the last Mamluks hardly one had a Moslem father.

As the Mamluk sun was setting in the East, another Moslem star — that of the Ottoman Turks — was rising in the West. Sooner or later the two powers had to clash. Hostility found its first expression in encounters on the border line of Asia Minor and Syria. The major confrontation took place on August 24, 1516, on a plain north of Aleppo named Marj Dabiq. The Turkish forces were led by the ninth Ottoman sultan, the energetic Salim I (1512–1520), while those of Egypt were headed by the aged forty-sixth sultan, al-Ghuri (1500–1516). At the first charge the Aleppo governor commanding the left wing treacherously deserted. Shortly after, al-Ghuri fell from his horse stricken with apoplexy. The Ottoman victory was decisive. Salim pushed south, encountered and routed Tuman-Bay, an ex-slave of al-Ghuri and his successor, in a battle outside Cairo (September 1519), captured the sultan, and hanged him on one of the capital's main gates. The Ottoman victor returned to Constantinople proudly including in his entourage the nominal caliph, heir of the one installed by Baybars. Cairo, for centuries seat of Eastern Islam, assumed in an emerging Ottoman Empire the status of a provincial capital, and so remained for centuries.

Misr al-Qahirah, the dissident capital, rival of Baghdad and for a time greatest center of Islamic culture and power, checked the advance of the Mongol wave and dealt the final blows to Crusading Syria and Palestine.

6

Cordova:

The European Capital

Cordova surpasses all cities of the world in four principal features: its bridge over the Guadalquivir, its mosque, its palace al-Zahra' and, above all, the sciences cultivated therein.

Al-Maqqari

*T*he Romans called it Corduba, the Spaniards Córdoba, and the Arabs Qurtubah. Earlier the Phoenicians conjecturally named it Qaryat-tub. Had any Semitists been in the company of the Arab conquerors they might have suspected the Semitic origin of the name and given the city its corresponding form in Arabic, Qaryah Tayyibah, rather than Arabicizing its Latin form.

The conjectured original name meant the "good town," and a good town Cordova was. Situated on the right bank of the Baetis River, at the foot of the Sierra Morena, the city had easy access southward through Seville to the Mediterranean and northward by the great commercial highway named after Augustus Caesar, Via Augusta. The Baetis after the Arab conquest became Guadalquivir, a corruption of Arabic al-Wadi al-Kabir (the great river), an etymology perhaps more difficult to detect than that of Corduba from Qaryat-tub. Cordova's natural resources of water, climate, soil, and situation gave it a high potential of development realized only once in its long and checkered history.

The city created by early Semites reached its height under medieval Semites. From its earliest days coins in Phoenician characters have

135

survived; they were followed by coins in the modified form known as Punic originating in Carthage. It was Hamilcar Barca, distinguished father of a more distinguished son (Hannibal), who in 237 B.C. incorporated southern Spain (Andalusia, after the Vandals who overran it in the fifth Christian century) in his rising Carthaginian empire. Rome wrested Cordova from Carthage. In its more than six and a half centuries of Roman rule beginning in 152 B.C., Corduba had the distinction of achieving the status of the first Roman colony outside Italy. It also served as seat of a province bearing the river's name. Meantime it gave birth to a few intellectuals headed by the philosopher-statesman Seneca (ca. 4 B.C.–A.D. 65). In 45 B.C. Julius Caesar destroyed about half of the town and slaughtered some 20,000 of its inhabitants for having supported the sons of his rival Pompey.

The substitution of Visigothic for Roman rule accelerated rather than retarded the city's decline. Originally a horde of Teutonic barbarians the Visigoths, though partially Romanized, perpetuated certain traditional institutions of their own, adopted the Arian form of Christianity — considered a heresy by their Roman Catholic subjects — and established a new caste system topped by royalty, nobility, and clergy and based on serfs and slaves. The Jews, an abused and disgruntled sizable minority, struck another discordant note. They provided collaborationists to the Arab invaders as their coreligionists had done in Syria. Toledo after Seville served as the main Visigothic capital. Visigothic rule was punctuated by destructive raids from other Teutonic hordes and by internal disturbances and dynastic disputes. Of the twenty-three Visigothic kings from 531 to 711 (the year of Moslem conquest), five were murdered and one was deposed.

It was during the Arab period, particularly under the Umayyads (756–1031), that Qurtubah enjoyed its prime and grandeur and took its place as the most civilized city in Western Europe. None of the other Spanish historic cities — Toledo, Seville, and Granada — approached it in material prosperity and intellectual attainments. When Christendom was deep in its Dark Ages, Moslem Cordova was rearing men, evolving ideas, writing books, erecting buildings, and producing works of art that constituted a unique civilization. In the West it had one peer in Constantinople and in the East another, Baghdad. At no time before or after did any Spanish city enjoy such distinction.

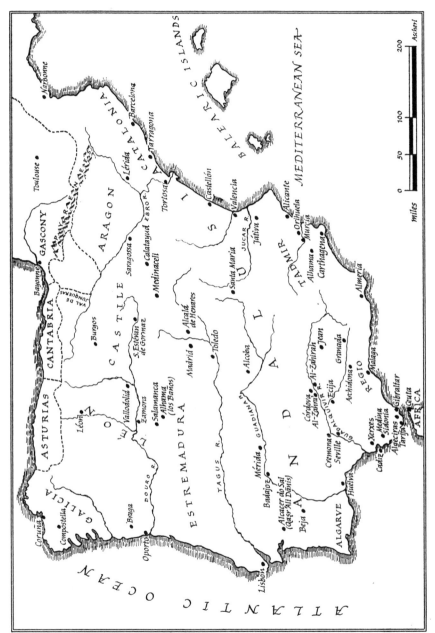

Moslem Spain

CORDOVA

I

The spectacular Arab invasion of Spain, it may be recalled, beginning 711 by Tariq and 712 by Musa ibn-Nusayr, netted in short seven years the bulk of the Iberian Peninsula. It was followed by the dramatic escape in 750 of the nineteen-year old 'Abd-al-Rahman and his equally spectacular triumphal march through al-Andalus culminating in the capture of Cordova in 756. The future Umayyad capital had been first acquired in October 711 (following the decisive victory over the Visigothic king Roderick) after a two-month siege. The treachery of a shepherd who pointed out a breach in the city wall facilitated the entry. But the city did not immediately begin its career as a capital. When in 714 Musa was recalled to Damascus he left his son 'Abd-al-'Aziz as governor with Seville as his seat. Five years later al-Samh ibn-Malik al-Khawlani transferred the seat to Cordova and rebuilt the Roman bridge over the Guadalquivir; he also made a fresh survey of the land for taxation purposes. From Cordova al-Samh conducted military campaigns ending (719) in the capture of Narbonne, in southern France, near the Mediterranean. His attempt the following year at Toulouse, where he suffered "martyrdom," was a failure. Cordova's governor (amir) at the advent of 'Abd-al-Rahman, Yusuf al-Fihri, was not eager to be replaced; he tried to satisfy the pretender with gifts including his daughter's hand. The victory of the newcomer (al-dakhil, which became a sobriquet of 'Abd-al-Rahman) over al-Fihri May 15, 756, made him nominally the governor general of Moslem Spain. The following year he discontinued the mention of the 'Abbasid name in the Friday sermon, but did not substitute his own. He and his immediate successors, till the rise of 'Abd-al-Rahman III, ruled as independent amirs. Spain thus became the first province to cut itself entirely from caliphal headquarters.

It was not long, however, before 'Abd-al-Rahman discovered that even a nominally independent governor was not necessarily a real governor and that conquering a country may be easier than ruling it. His realm was, and remained for long, rent asunder along not only political but religious, racial, and nationalist lines. The dual character of the population and its Christian-Moslem polarization was not the only problem. Among the Moslems, Sunnites were in conflict with Shi'ites. North Arabians continued to cherish their traditional feud with South Arabians. Pro-Umayyads stood in opposition to pro-'Abbasids. Berbers, who spearheaded the invasion, felt that the Arabs parcelled out the smiling plains of al-Andalus among themselves leaving them the leftover, an arid, ill-watered, windswept central area. Nor were the Berbers united. They were split into two camps, sedentary

The Quadalquivir with Cordova in background, ca. 1900
Eugene Schmidt, *Cordove et Grenade* (Paris, 1902)

and nomadic, with varying outlooks on life and differing interests. Those of them who fought with 'Abd-al-Rahman at the conquest of Cordova never forgave him for having declared general amnesty in his consideration for the rights of private property, thus depriving the victors of the usual privilege of looting. The fallen governor's harem were accorded by 'Abd-al-Rahman honorable treatment and their pillaged valuables were restored.

In the Umayyad tradition al-Dakhil pursued with his Christian subjects a policy of tolerance beyond the contemporary standard, dealt leniently with those of his people he thought could be won over and ruthlessly with others. The fugitive al-Fihri, who in Toledo, the proud

139

"royal city," headed a rebellious movement, was finally captured and decapitated. His head was exhibited on Cordova's bridge. Other rebellious heads, as they popped up Hydra-like over the land, were equally crushed.

The challenge to the new order was not limited to the local scene. Al-Mansur could not stand idly by while the western wing of his 'Abbasid empire was being amputated by an Umayyad upstart. In 763 he ordered his governor general in Qayrawan, al-'Ala' ibn-Mughith, to proceed against the new enemy. On the battlefield north of Seville seven hundred of the invaders were slaughtered and the head of their leader, wrapped in the caliph's diploma of appointment, was dispatched to al-Mansur, then pilgrimaging at Mecca. As he opened the mysterious package, the caliph reportedly exclaimed, "Praise be to Allah for putting the sea between us and that kind of a foe." On another occasion al-Mansur did not agree with his courtiers who, in reply to a question posed by him as to who the falcon of Quraysh was, had named three: Mu'awiyah, 'Abd-al-Malik, and himself. He insisted it was none other than the young Umayyad fugitive who, after five years of wandering in the deserts of Syria and North Africa and without the benefit of an army, friends, or money, succeeded in establishing an empire on European soil and defying the 'Abbasid authority.

In 778 a new foe, Charlemagne, king of the Franks and emperor of the West, appeared on the scene, in response to an invitation from disaffected Moslem governors headed by al-Fihri's son-in-law and other chiefs of Barcelona and Saragossa. Charlemagne's large-scale military expedition into northeastern Spain resulted in utter failure. The destruction of his retreating army by the Basques in the Pyrenees and the death of his paladin Roland gave rise to a large body of early medieval literature including the celebrated French epic titled *Chanson de Roland*. 'Abd-al-Rahman thereupon entered Saragossa (Saraqustah) without striking a blow. But that made no difference. The amir of Cordova was now generally recognized as the hero of Islam, the match of the mightiest Christian ruler in the West and the mightiest Moslem ruler in the East. As for the self-confidence the victory generated in the Dakhil, it had no bounds. If we can believe his biographers, he contemplated a naval invasion to reclaim his ancestral domain, a plan that was not executed. For twenty-two years he had been in a state of war. It was time for a respite.

'Abd-al-Rahman the administrator was no less distinguished than 'Abd-al-Rahman the warrior. The governmental setup he worked out was modeled after that of his ancestors in Damascus and adapted to local needs. In his person as an independent amir all authority — military, political, financial — was concentrated and could be relegated to aides or governors. In the exercise of his functions he was assisted by a chamberlain (*hajib*). Under the chamberlain there developed in due course bureaus of finance, military affairs, and interior affairs, each under a secretary. The Visigothic provincial divisions were maintained, with slight modifications, and each was put under a governor (*wali*) for political, military, and financial affairs. Each province had a judge (*qadi*) for religious and legal matters. The Cordova judge stood out as the superior. The amir surrounded himself with a bodyguard from Black Africa, and built up an army of 40,000 mercenaries recruited mainly from Slavonians sold by their German captors in the north and brought into the Cordova market by Jewish traders. They constituted a pillar of strength for the new state. Land forces were supplemented by sea forces, the country being exposed to naval attack on three sides. Under his late successor 'Abd-al-Rahman III the Moslem navy dominated the western Mediterranean.

In accordance with koranic law Dhimmi Christians and Jews were subject, additional to the land-tax (*kharaj*), to a poll-tax graduated from twelve to forty-eight dirhams, depending on the financial ability of the individual. Taxes could be paid in cash or in kind. Women and children, priests and slaves, the disabled and the diseased were generally exempt. That the change from Visigothic to Moslem rule involved no worsening of the condition of the indigenous population is the view held by most modern scholars. In fact, it may have ameliorated it, particularly in the case of Jews and the servile class. The Jews were natural allies. The new faith provided members of the discontented servile class with a means of escape. By embracing it serfs acquired economic advantages, and slaves were entitled to full freedom at least from their Christian masters, for no non-Moslem could enslave a Moslem. In due course members of the higher social classes, including landowners, sought relief from taxation by abjuring their faith. A few may have become secret Christians. A large Visigothic family in the north, the banu-Qasi, adopted Islam and in the ninth century played an important role in national affairs. To the conquerors, however, Spain was a land to exploit rather than convert, and initially no zeal for proselytizing was manifested.

It was not long before the prosperous reputation of the new European capital of Islam began to attract flocks of fortune seekers and ambitious emigrants from western Asia and northern Africa. Relatives of the amir were the first to rush. Meantime the number of Neo-Moslems (sing. *Muwallad*) was mounting by leaps and bounds. Spain, be it remembered, was one of the last European countries to be Christianized, and at the time of the Moslem conquest many country districts were still pagan. Marriage was a major means of integration. Fair-skinned, blue-eyed, golden-haired Gothic and Spanish women were especially attractive to the newcomers, and Islam did not insist on the conversion of wives but laid claim to the children. The first governor of Moslem Spain, 'Abd-al-'Aziz son of Musa ibn-Nusayr, set the precedent by marrying Roderick's widow, but she insisted on making the door of her palace chapel so low that her husband had to bend on entering as if in an act of worship. Exaggerated rumors of his conversion to Christianity resulted in his murder in his capital Seville (716). 'Abd-al-Rahman also included in his harem a Christian wife, whose son Hisham he designated as heir apparent.

It was time to symbolize the majesty of the new religion, embodied in the majesty of the new state, in a structure comparable in grandeur to the European cathedrals and competitive in attractiveness to the Meccan Kaabah, then in hostile hands. Hitherto a political capital, Cordova had to become a religious capital. The site chosen was that of a Visigothic cathedral on an earlier Roman temple. The building began in 785, three years before 'Abd-al-Rahman's death, and cost in its first year 100,000 dinars. Occupying an area of 460 by 280 feet and encircled by a high, thick battlement flanked by buttresses of watch-towers, it was provided with marble columns partly from Roman monuments to support graceful double arches. The standard height of a column was thirteen feet and some were decorated by later caliphs with gold and lapis lazuli. The ensemble resembled a stately forest of pillars. Seemingly indestructible pine wood, carved and painted, overlaid the ceilings. Colorful chandeliers, partly from church bells, turned the night into day. Mural decorations by artists from Syria and Persia added to the glamor. Eleven doors from a spacious outer court led the

Albert F. Calvert, *Moorish Remains in Spain* (London & New York, 1906)

Colonnade of the Grand Mosque of Cordova as a cathedral, 1780

worshipers inside. The undertaking was too big for one man to complete. The amir's son and successor Hisham I (788–796) carried on and added a minaret. Hisham's grandson 'Abd-al-Rahman II (822–852) enlarged the building and enriched the decorations of the doors and

143

windows. The final and crowning touches were administered by the third 'Abd-al-Rahman and his successor al-Hakam II.

Before starting the structure the founder of the Umayyad dynasty in Spain had launched a number of secular and religious building projects. His inspiration may have come from his predecessors, originators of the earliest monumental structures in Islam. Chroniclers credit 'Abd-al-Rahman I with improving the aqueduct supplying the capital with its water, enlarging the Guadalquivir bridge, and renovating the fifty-year-old city fortifications. For his own residence he built two miles outside the capital a villa with a garden enriched with exotic trees and flowers. He named it al-Rusafah in nostalgic remembrance of a country seat near the Euphrates where he had spent his earlier and happier days. Tradition credits him with having introduced among other fruits and trees a special kind of pomegranate and of date palm. To the palm he, a poet like many other amirs, addressed a touching poem:

> O Palm, thou art a stranger in the West,
>   Far from thy Orient home unblest.
> Weep! But thou canst not. Dumb, dejected tree,
>   Thou art not made to sympathize with me.
> Ah, thou wouldst weep, if thou hadst tears to pour,
>   For thy companions on Euphrates' shore,
> But yonder tall groves thou rememberest not,
>   As I, in hating foes, have my old friends forgot.[1]

'Abd-al-Rahman began his amirate in the style of the founder of the Umayyad dynasty in Damascus but ended it in that of the founder of the 'Abbasid dynasty in Baghdad. The harrowing experiences turned the wine of life in his veins into vinegar. As he advanced in age he became more suspicious and more tyrannical. One after the other of his aides, confidants, and relatives fell from grace. His freedman Badr, whose assistance in the flight from Syria was invaluable and who had served as emissary to Spain and was rewarded with a high office, was finally deprived of his property and banished. Reason: failure to continue his early servility. One of the two Arab chiefs to whom the amir owed his throne was beheaded and the other came near meeting the

---

1. Reynold A. Nicholson, *A Literary History of the Arabs* (Cambridge, reprint 1969), p. 418.

Albert F. Calvert, *Moorish Remains in Spain* (London & New York, 1906)

Main entrance of Grand Mosque of Cordova, 1780

same fate. Two Umayyad princes who were caught plotting against him were executed. But the deepest cut of all was the execution of his own nephew. For long the memory of the tragedy haunted the unhappy old man. "How can my eye," he was once heard to say, "meet my brother's eye after having deprived him of his only offspring." He thereupon handed a courtier 5,000 dinars, ordering him to offer it to his bereft brother and request him to go anywhere beyond the frontiers of the realm.

II

In the period between the reigns of the first and the third 'Abd-al-Rahmans — under whom Cordova enjoyed its greatest measure of might and splendor — the capital experienced civil and religious disturbances that carried it to the brink of anarchy. As long as 'Abd-al-Rahman I's pious and scholarly son Hisham (788–796) ruled everything was quiet. But trouble began after him and continued until the rise of 'Abd-al-Rahman III in 912. Unlike his father, Hisham's son

145

al-Hakam I (796–822) was a frivolous winebibber, more interested in hunting than in administering state affairs. Not only his conduct but that of his foreign mercenaries and bodyguard were an irritant to his orthodox subjects including the Muwallads. By his time so numerous had these Neo-Moslems (renegades, from the Christian point of view) become in the city that they fully occupied a southern quarter (rabad) of it. The Muwallads had their own reason for discontent. Many of them, sons of slaves and serfs, worked as laborers and mechanics. The equality with the old Moslems they sought proved more theoretical than practical. A large body had fallen under the influence of excessively zealous Berber theologians who had their own ax to grind.

As al-Hakam was one day passing in a street a Muwallad mob hurled stones at him while their Berber mentors applauded. Seventy-two of the ringleaders were apprehended and crucified. Another attack staged on the royal palace by insurgents was ruthlessly repulsed by the cavalry. Three hundred leaders were nailed to crosses, heads downwards. In three days the entire quarter was leveled to the ground and its inhabitants scattered. Eight hundred families found asylum in the newly built Moroccan capital Fas (Fez); others, numbering some fifteen thousand, landed at Alexandria; still others wandered to Crete, where they started a Moslem dynasty. A part of Crete then belonged to Byzantium. The victory won by the amir was indeed at a high price to the city.

Alongside the Muwallads there emerged in the reign of al-Hakam's son 'Abd-al-Rahman II (822–852) — who was no improvement on his father — a curious, somewhat unique class known as Musta'rib (Ar. for "would-be Arab," Sp. Mozarab). These were Spanish Christians who, dazzled by the glamor of Moslem culture, lured by the Arabic language, and attracted by the harem institution, adopted the new language and customs but persisted in the exercise of their traditional faith. Political influence usually leaves a corresponding cultural influence. A contemporary Christian writer of Cordova deplored how his fellow citizens, intoxicated with the eloquence of the foreign tongue, shunned the works of the Latin Fathers.

With the increase of Musta'ribs in numbers, the Christian reaction increased. The anti-Arabicization movement found a leader in a zealous, ascetic priest named Eulogius supported by a wealthy friend. The movement had its first martyr in another Cordovan cleric, Perfectus.

On the feast of Ramadan in 850 Perfectus was publicly executed for having cursed Muhammad and reviled Islam, knowing well what the consequences would be. Nothing could have better solidified the movement. The martyr soon became a saint and stories about miracles performed by him were circulated. Shortly after this episode a monk, appearing in court on the pretext of desiring to profess Islam, vehemently execrated it and suffered the supreme penalty. The race for voluntary martyrdom began. It assumed the proportions of hysteria that caught clergy and lay men and women. For years aspirants for the holy death contended to force often reluctant judges to pass execution judgment on them. In less than two months eleven Cordovans experienced self-immolation. In vain did the council of bishops, at the instigation of 'Abd-al-Rahman, issue decrees forbidding the practice.

Two pathetic cases were those of a lovely maiden named Flora, child of a mixed marriage, and an equally youthful nun, Mary, sister of a decapitated cleric. The two were friends and vowed to die together. A compassionate judge sent them to jail in the hope that they might recant. At times they must have faltered in their determination to mount the scaffold, but then there was Eulogius, also in jail, ready to administer the counter doses of enthusiasm — despite his love, puritanical, for Flora. Death for Christ in the hope of gaining eternal life was represented as preferable to natural death. On November 24, 851, the two virgins paid the high price. The movement did not subside till eight years later when 'Abd-al-Rahman's successor Muhammad (852–886) decapitated Eulogius. By then the "martyrs of Cordova" had numbered forty-four.

The destruction of the Muwallads and the repression of the Christians in the capital did not solve the problems. Disturbances, civil and religious, not only spread throughout the amirate but acquired momentum as they spread. As the Christian-Moslem tension mounted, disenchanted second-class citizens, hitherto passive, became active. In the north the independent state of Aragon, under the banu-Qasi, incorporated in the mid-ninth century into itself Saragossa. The formerly Christian banu-Qasi allied themselves with their neighbors to the west, the Christian kings of Leon. Toledo, which throughout Umayyad domination was more in rebellion than in peace, fell prey to a Berber family. Seville, once center of Roman and Visigothic culture and now largely populated by descendants of Romans and Visigoths, broke off under an Arab family. More ominous was the situation in the south. Here a Moslem named ibn-Hafsun, scion of a Visigothic count, started his colorful career about 880 by organizing a band of brigands and operating from a castle at the foot of Mount Babastro. Posing as the champion of a long-suppressed nationality he found ready supporters among disgruntled peasants of Elvira, Jaen, and other neighboring towns. As his domain extended he professed (899) the religion of his forebears, assuming the baptismal name of Samuel. He even negotiated with Baghdad for recognition as sultan of Spain. Thus the dawn of the tenth century found Cordova isolated, its throne shaky, and the Umayyad state on the brink of collapse — an eventuality averted by one man.

III

That man was 'Abd-al-Rahman III. He was the one destined not only to save the state but to raise it to a height hitherto unattained. His were those qualities of energy, resoluteness, and intelligence that characterize men who achieve greatness. Under him (912–961) and his son al-Hakam II (961–976), al-Andalus enjoyed its prime of affluence, fame, and influence.

When the twenty-three–year–old amir assumed power, his authority hardly extended beyond the capital and its environs. The principal towns were under local governors or rebel leaders, all in a state bordering on anarchy. The countryside swarmed with brigands. So dangerous was internal communication that seven years are known to have passed without a single caravan venturing between Cordova and Saragossa. The new monarch's immediate task was to reclaim the lost territory, pacify it, and unite it. Ecija, a few miles southwest of the capital, was reduced before the year was over. Carmona near Seville followed. Archidona offered no resistance. Before the end of the next year, Seville, a competitor of Cordova, opened its gates. The death in 917 of ibn-Hafsun removed out of the way a formidable foe of thirty-seven years' standing. But his followers held out in their mountain fortresses of Regio until one after the other was forced to submit. Mighty Bobastro, garrisoned by his sons, was stormed in 928. Only proud Toledo remained defiant. Four years later it succumbed to famine and a two-year siege. For the first time in more than half a century the amir of al-Andalus was one in more than name.

Engaged as he was in domestic problems 'Abd-al-Rahman could not be blind to two other threatening dangers: one from the north where native Christians were asserting their independence and forming states, and the other from the south where the Fatimids were expanding their influence and domain. In 909, it will be recalled, 'Ubaydullah al-Mahdi established his Shi'i caliphate as a rival to that of Sunni Baghdad and was now stretching his arm westward. In 929 the amir of Cordova took the fateful step and assumed the exalted title of *al-Khalifah al-Nasir li-Din Allah* (the caliph-defender of the religion of Allah). For the first time the world of Islam was treated to the sight of three rival caliphs, two of whom were orthodox. In 931 the forces of the new caliph occupied Ceuta and used it as a base. For years thereafter Morocco served as a bone of contention between the two expanding rival powers.

More serious and complicated was the problem generated by the emerging Christian states on the northern border. At the advent of Islam, Asturias, the mountainous region along the Bay of Biscay west of the Basque region in the Pyrenees, provided shelter for fleeing Visigoths. By this time it had expanded, achieved union with its western neighbor Leon, and developed into a center of resistance and aggression. As the amirate of Cordova deteriorated, Asturias and its southeastern neighbor Navarre progressed. Pillaging forays into the south became successive and wars to regain lost territory successful. This was especially true during the reign of Alfonso III, king of Leon and Asturias from 866 to 910, whose military exploits in Moslem territory earned him the surname of great. In 917 a successor of Alfonso captured one of 'Abd-al-Rahman's generals and nailed his head with that of a wild boar to the wall of a frontier fortress.

It was time for the amir to take the field in person. This was not only his religious but his political duty as well. The fact that he was son of a Christian mother made no difference. In his first campaign of 920 he penetrated through the debatable land between Islam and Christianity, demolished several enemy fortresses, and inflicted a severe defeat on the combined forces of the kings of Galicia (west of Leon through Portugal) and Navarre. Four years later he conducted a second campaign reaching Pampelona (Pamplona), fortified capital of Navarre, which he demolished. Navarre after Asturias had become a bulwark of Christianity. Incursions in both directions continued until 939. In that year the joint forces of Leon and Navarre inflicted on 'Abd-al-Rahman the first major defeat in his twenty-seven years of almost incessant war. At Alhandega (Ar. *al-khandaq*, the moat), a few miles southwest Salamanca, the caliph's huge army of over 50,000 was virtually annihilated and he, accompanied by a few horsemen, barely escaped with his life. The Christians of the north, however, plagued with internecine jealousies and interminable feuds, failed to press their advantage. Otherwise the history to-be might have been different from what it was. As for the caliph, he made no major attempt thereafter to expand northward. The boundary line for a time was stabilized. Roughly, it extended from the mouth of the Ebro to the Atlantic.

Three years before the battle of Alhandega the caliph began the construction of a residence worthy of himself. The site he chose was a spur of the Sierra Morena three miles northwest of Cordova and overlooking the Guadalquivir. The name he gave it, al-Zahra' (the bright-faced), was that of a favorite concubine.

The building, we are assured, covered an area of 2,700 cubits by 1,500 cubits. The caliph spent the remaining twenty-five years of his reign building it, employing 10,000 daily laborers and 3,000 beasts of burden. So absorbed was he in the project that once for three successive weeks he missed the Friday prayer and was threatened by the preacher with hellfire in case he persisted. The cost per year was 300,-000 dinars, one third of the state revenue, the other two-thirds being devoted to the military and public works and to the reserve fund. The imperial palace could accommodate 6,314 women of various classes comprising the caliph's harem, and 3,752 bodyguard, eunuchs, and pages. The bodyguard headed an army of 100,000 men, mostly slaves of Christian origin purchased young, Arabicized, and Islamized. Arab chroniclers, geographers, and poets drew heavily on their stores of rhetoric and eloquence in describing this marvel of architecture. It had no equal in the West or the East. Only al-Hamra' (Alhambra) of later days could match it. Its 4,000 columns of marble and gold were brought from Carthage, Rome, and Constantinople; some were received as presents. The Carthage columns may be looked upon as a gift from a mother to embellish her daughter. A principal donor of this and other valuable gifts was the Byzantine emperor. The reception hall had walls and roofs of marble ornamented with gold, windows of transparent alabaster, eight gilded doors set with ivory and ebony and bearing precious stones. It featured in its midst a unique basin of quicksilver which sent lightning-like flashes as the sunrays passing through the doors hit it.

The caliphal court was dazzling in more than one way. As the accredited envoys of the monarchs of Byzantium, Italy, Germany, and of other states were officially received, they were treated with pompous ceremony and a display of Arab hospitality and courtesy that left an enduring impression. On one occasion when the caliph was giving audience to Byzantine envoys, he called upon a visiting professor of philology from Baghdad, abu-'Ali al-Qali, to deliver the oration. Struck with stage fright, the renowned orator could not proceed beyond the introductory formula of praise to Allah and blessing on His Prophet. Whereupon the caliph called on another scholar who extemporized a most eloquent address covering pages — all in rhymed prose. Another notable occasion involved Queen Regent Theuda (Tota) of Navarre, whose forces had earlier taken part in the humiliation of 'Abd-al-Rahman on the battlefield. In 957 the queen appealed to the caliph for aid to restore her grandson Sancho the Fat to the Leonese throne, which he had lost because of his corpulence. So fat was Sancho that he could not walk without support. 'Abd-al-Rahman stipulated that she should first restore certain border fortresses and then appear in person. This she did, accompanied by her king-son and grandson. The royal guests were received in state, the victim of corpulence was relieved of his affliction by the court's Jewish physician and counselor Hasday ben-Shaprut, and returned (960) through the caliph's efforts to his former position.

Work on al-Zahra' continued under 'Abd-al-Rahman's successor, al-Hakam II. Meantime courtiers and dignitaries had constructed palaces and offices around the royal palace, converting the whole into a town (Madinat al-Zahra'). The decline, however, began immediately thereafter. Al-Hakam's successor had a powerful vizir who built for himself (978–980) a magnificent residence south of the capital and gave his functionaries land to build domiciles around it. This he named al-Madinah al-Zahirah (the brilliantly flourishing city). Al-Zahirah supplanted al-Zahra'. As it fell into disuse, al-Zahra' was suffered to crumble. Under the stern rule of the Berber al-Mohads (sing. *muwahhid*), some fifty years after its completion, its ruin was complete. Part of its material was later used for building a nearby monastery. Recent excavations failed to yield enough to reveal the glory that was once al-Zahra'.

Al-Hakam's architectural contribution to the royal residence was dwarfed by that to the place of worship. Under pressure from a mounting population in the capital he extended the building ninety-five feet north to south and an equal number east to west. He then added colonades, a pulpit, a bower (*maqsurah*) reserved for his use when not serving as a prayer leader, and a mihrab, the third in the building. The columns, some of marble, porphyry, and jasper, numbered eight hundred and fifty. The pulpit was reportedly constructed of 35,000 pieces of ivory and choice wood fastened with silver and gold pins and encrusted with precious stones. The maqsurah was also lavishly embellished, but it was the mihrab with its exquisite decoration and koranic inscriptions that won the prize. The mihrab walls were inlaid in mosaic and its roof was formed of a single block of white marble carved in the shape of a shell. This is the only equipment that has survived in its entirety.

Before al-Hakam the mosque was the beneficiary of several patrons but after him only one, his successor's vizir, bestowed special care on it using material from churches he had destroyed in the north. By this time its interior yielded in size only to St. Peter in Christendom and the Mecca Mosque in Islam. The seemingly interminable series of aisles, spanned by low, painted arches made the mosque seem larger. Both capital and mosque received the first serious blow in 1031 at the collapse of the Umayyad caliphate. None of the succeeding dynasties seemed to have had sufficient interest to maintain it properly, to say nothing about renovating it. It had then been in use for two and a half centuries. It received its fatal blow in 1236 when Ferdinand III, king of Castile and Leon, conquered Cordova and converted it into a cathedral. Repeated alterations, especially after the early sixteenth century when the remaining Moslems had been expelled from the land, impaired but did not destroy the original character of the building, deserving the name by which it came to be known, La Mezquita. Its conversion assured its longevity. Hardly any other monumental

Vertical section of the dome and cupola of the mihrab, Grand Mosque of Cordova

Cordova structure, including al-Zahra' and al-Zahirah, has left a trace. The old place of worship remains with al-Hamra' as one of the two chief Moslem attractions to tourists.

Under al-Hakam the capital city rose to new heights in military power. Five years after his accession he forced the king of Castile and Leon and the king of Navarre to sign a treaty of peace. He later repulsed a naval attack on Lisbon by Normans (from Denmark), occupied Tangier, and took the Idrisi king of Morocco as prisoner. The removal of the Fatimid capital from Tunisia to the newly built (969) Cairo facilitated his task. Tangier served as a base for future operations eastward. Al-Hakam's claim to fame, however, rests in an entirely different field, that of learning. Not only did he patronize scholars but he was a scholar in his own right. In fact some consider him the greatest caliphal scholar Islam produced. He is credited with founding twenty-seven free schools in his capital, endowing chairs in the university started by 'Abd-al-Rahman I in conjunction with the mosque, inviting professors to it from the East, and enriching it with a library unequalled in contents. In quest of manuscripts his agents ransacked the bookshops of Egypt, Syria, and Iraq. The university library came to possess 400,-000 volumes catalogued in forty books. The caliph maintained a private collection in the palace and left in his own hand marginal notes on some of its contents. For the acquisition of a first copy of *Kitab al-Aghani* (book of songs) by al-Isbahani of Aleppo, a descendant of the last Umayyad caliph, al-Hakam sent a thousand dinars.

Other than Islamic sciences, the university featured mathematics, astronomy, philosophy, and medicine. It attracted foreign students, Christian and Moslem, and contributed to making Cordova a world intellectual center. When Christian rulers in the north needed a surgeon, an architect, or a musician, it was to the Moslem capital that they turned. The court physician of al-Hakam was abu-al-Qasim (Lat. Abulcasis) al-Zahrawi (d. 1013), the outstanding surgeon of Islam. Al-Zahrawi's work on surgery describes cauterization of wounds and crushing stones in the bladder; it emphasizes the importance of vivisection as well as dissection and has illustrations of instruments he used which helped lay the foundation of European surgery. Translated into Latin at Toledo by Gerard of Cremona (d. 1187), his book passed through numerous editions including one in Venice (1497), another in Basel (1541), and a third in Oxford as late as 1778. A contemporary and fellow Cordovan of al-Zahrawi was al-Majriti (d. 1007), the earliest scientist of importance in Moslem Spain. Al-Majriti revised the planetary tables (*zij*) of al-Khwarizmi and his work was translated (1126) in Toledo into Latin by Adelard of Bath.

Cordova dazzled other than Moslem eyes. Though commenting on the martyrdom of Eulogius, a contemporary nun in distant Germany referred to the city as the "jewel of the world, young and exquisite,

Albert F. Calvert, *Moorish Remains in Spain* (London & New York, 1906)

La Mezquita, 1780

proud in its might." Centuries later eminent English scholars like
Adelard of Bath and Roger Bacon were still advising European students to attend Moslem schools in preference to native ones. Besides
the university library, Arab statisticians assure us the city boasted 37
libraries, numberless bookstores, 800 public schools, and 600 mosques.
They add 150 hospitals, 900 public baths, 600 inns, 80,455 shops, 130,-
000 houses (other than those for functionaries), and a total population
of 300,000. Its people enjoyed a high standard of living and refinement
and walked on paved streets reflecting at night light from bordering
houses — all this at a time when hardly a town in Europe, Constantinople excepted, counted more than a few thousand inhabitants. Pari-
sians and Londoners were still trudging on muddy, dark alleys, and
scholars in Oxford and Paris were viewing bathing as a heathen practice.

Another field in which the Moslem metropolis established international reputation was that of industrial arts. By the tenth century
there were centered in it schools of ivory and wood carving, ceramics,
glass, and metalwork. How could the decorations of the Mosque, al-
Zahra', and al-Zahirah have been achieved without them? Specimens
of caskets and boxes partly or wholly of ivory, with carved inlaid and
painted ornamentation, from the tenth and subsequent centuries, are
treasured in museums of our day. Cordovan artists in glassware and

155

brassware and in inlaying steel and other metals built upon a heritage from the East and bequeathed their tradition to the West. Among those who played a major role as culture carriers were the Mozarabs, who, we learned before, were enchanted with Arab art, language, song, and music and had by this time adopted the Arabic tongue and other Moslem aspects of life while retaining their Christian faith. Some used double personal names, even practiced circumcision and kept harem. In such cities as Cordova, Toledo, and later Granada, they became so numerous as to constitute a distinct social class occupying special quarters. Then came that remnant of the Moslem community which remained in Spain after the *reconquista* and in due course were assimilated. They came to be known as Mudejars (sing. *mudajjan*, domesticated), developed styles of their own and left specimens of pottery which modern collectors rank only below the Chinese. In architecture Mudajjan workmen merged Christian and Moslem traditions to produce a special form of the horseshoe and vault that became the national style of Spain. In Islam the round horseshoe arch appears first in the Umayyad Mosque of Damascus; in Spain it undoubtedly existed before the Moslem conquest. But it was Cordovan architects who fully realized the structural and decorative possibilities of the arch and put it into wide use. It became known as the Moorish arch. But the system of vaulting involving intersecting arches and visible intersecting ribs was an original Cordovan Moslem contribution.

Weaving was another industry centered in Cordova but spread over the land. Oriental silk textiles, rich in color and in floral and geometric designs, found favor with the European royalty and aristocracy for robes. Even churches made a limited use of them for vestments and wrappings of saintly relics. As early as the twelfth century European weavers began to adopt Islamic designs. They later started to imitate the Arabic script for merely decorative purposes. Tanning and embossing leather was another industry in which Cordovans excelled. As it passed on to Morocco, France, and England it left linguistic fossils in the words *morocco, cordovan, cordwain,* and *cordwainer.*

IV

The death of al-Hakam ushered in an era of dark ages for Cordova, an era in which only one bright spot stands out the military career of his successor's chamberlain. When the twelve-year-old Hisham II (976–1009) succeeded his father, he became and remained puppet of a powerful vizir-chamberlain (*hajib*) Muhammad ibn-'Amir. Originally one guarding the door or access to the ruler, the hajib in Spain became superior to the vizir and served as liaison between caliph and vizirs. The ambitious ibn-'Amir began life as a humble scribe and became a favorite protégé of Hisham's beautiful Basque mother. For seventeen years he managed to rule Spain as a caliph in all but name. Not only was he able to ingratiate himself with the queen-mother but with the theologians, by burning all books on philosophy and other subjects blacklisted by them, and with the poets, by bounteous subsidies. What was of more consequence was his reorganization of the army on a firmer regimental basis and raising its standard of training and discipline. He recruited it largely from slaves and mercenaries of Negro, Berber, and European Christian origin. The preoccupation of the Fatimids in the problems of the East, and of the Leonese and Castilians in the endless conflicts of the north gave him his opportunity. After the two 'Abd-al-Rahmans he became the third and last hero of militant Islam in Spain. In 981, the year after occupying al-Zahirah, the symbol of his independence in state affairs, ibn-'Amir assumed the royal title of al-Mansur bi-Allah (the one rendered victorious through Allah) and ordered it inscribed on the coins and cited in the Friday prayers. No more appropriate surname could he have chosen. Year after year al-Mansur led his troops triumphantly along the northwestern coast of Africa as well as through the northern part of the Iberian Peninsula east to west. In 985 he sacked Barcelona on the Mediterranean coast; three years later he razed the city of Leon with its massive walls and high towers. Among other cities he captured were Pamplona and Zamora. In 997 al-Mansur ventured through the mountainous passes into St. Iago (Santiago) de Compostella in northwestern Portugal and demolished its shrine. The place had become a favorite pilgrim resort since the ninth century for allegedly containing the relics of St. James the Great. On his triumphal return home the procession featured Christian captives bearing church doors and bells to be used in the mosque and other buildings. In 1002 he died as he wished while on a campaign in Castile, the fiftieth of his semiannual campaigns. In his coffin was buried the accumulated dust on his coat of mail. On his tomb the poet engraved this epitaph:

CORDOVA

His story in his relics you may trace
As tho' he stood before you face to face.
Never will Time bring his peer again,
Nor one to guard, like him,
the gaps [frontier forts] of Spain.[2]

But the monkish obituary writer had a different version: "In 1002 died Almanzor and was buried in hell."

None of the seven successors of al-Hakam in the fifty-five years (976–1031) after his death seem to have possessed any of those qualities of determination, energy, vitality, power of creativity, and the sense of permanence which produced the Cordovan caliphate and established the monumental edifices of worship, residence, and learning. One of them distinguished himself by destroying al-Zahirah. Clearly the "bride of al-Andalus" was entering upon its old age. Throughout, the military — Arabs, slaves, or Berbers — were in control. Hisham II (976–1009, 1010–1013) was installed and deposed twice; three of his successors held the throne more than once. Two caliphs met violent deaths. Pretenders to the caliphate appeared Berberized but claiming descent from the Prophet.

Disgusted, Cordovans and viziers took matters into their hands, shut up the fifty-five–year-old caliph Hisham III (1027–1031) with his family in a dismal vault attached to the mosque, and proclaimed the rule of a council of state in the form of a republic. When the epoch-making event was announced to the wretched caliph, all he asked for was a morsel of bread for his starving infant daughter.

The extinction of the caliphate doomed its capital to continued deterioration. A rash of short-lived petty states covered the face of the land. They bickered one with the other and ultimately fell easy preys to the rising Christian kingdoms of the north or to newly created Berber states from the south. The initial primacy lay with the kingdom of Seville, which in 1068 absorbed the Cordovan republic. Twenty three years later, Seville succumbed under the attack of Almoravids (sing. *murabit*, from *ribat*, fortified monastery), now holding sway from Senegal to Algiers. Of Berber origin, the Murabits embraced Islam with all the zeal of new converts. The marriage of sword and faith was, of course, not their innovation. Al-Andalus was incorporated

2. *Ibid.*, p. 413.

into their kingdom. Equally zealous but more vigorous were their kinsmen, the Muwahhids (unitarians) whose capital was the city of Morocco (Marrakush, Marrakesh), founded by them. In turn the Murabit gave way (1047) to the Muwahhids as masters of northwestern Africa and Moslem Spain. Like their predecessors the new rulers used Seville as a Spanish capital, whence they held the country for over a century and a half. In 1212 they suffered a disastrous defeat at the hands of a Christian army headed by Alfonso VIII of Castile assisted by the kings of Aragon and Navarre. The battle was fought seventy miles east of Cordova, where only one thousand of a Moslem army of "600,000" escaped to tell the tale. The overthrow of the Muwahhid dynasty left almost all Moslem Spain at the mercy of the conquerors. It was gradually parcelled out among Christian monarchs and local Moslem dynasts. In twenty-eight years after Alfonso's victory the main cities of Moslems, including Cordova (1236), were occupied. The fall of the capital and the transforming of its mosque ended a five-century career of Arabism and Islam. Only Granada in the deep south escaped to build al-Hamra' and revive for a time the glories of Cordova and Seville. By expulsion, conversion, and other means Cordova's Moslem population was annihilated. Its extinction was final and complete. No such tragedy had befallen any of its five forerunners in Asia and Africa.

V

The political eclipse of the Arab capital did not entail intellectual eclipse. Under the last caliphs as well as the Berber dynasties scholars maintained quantitively and qualitatively the level attained before. One of the earliest was 'Ali ibn-Hazm (994–1064), grandson of a Spanish convert, and one of the most original thinkers and prolific authors in Islam. Ibn-Hazm adorned in his youthful days the tottering courts of two caliphs and then retired to a life of scholarship. Some four hundred titles on theology and law, tradition and history, and allied subjects are ascribed to him. Best known of his extant works is *al-Fasl fi al-Milal w-al-Ahwa' w-al-Nihal* (the decisive work on sects, heterodoxies, and denominations), in which he treats Islam, Judaism, Christianity, and Zoroastrianism. In this first book on comparative religion, the author raises questions on biblical narratives that anticipate those raised by higher critics in the sixteenth century. In the field of medicine and its related subject botany, Muwahhid Cordova produced abu-Ja'far Ahmad al-Ghafiqi (d. 1165), whose collection of plants from Spain and Africa is considered the most thorough and accurate in classical Arabic. Its material was appropriated by his better-known countryman ibn-al-Baytar of Malaga (d. 1248). Interest in plants was then mainly for their medicinal value.

But the most influential thinker of this period, and one of the most influential in all periods of Islam, was the physician, philosopher, and scientist abu-al-Walid Muhammad ibn-Rushd (Averroës, 1126–1198). Ibn-Rushd served as a judge in Seville and in his place of nativity Cordova and flourished as a physician and consultant in the Muwahhid court of Morocco. In his medical encyclopedic work *al-Kulliyat fi al-Tibb* (generalities on medicine, corrupted into Lat. *Colliget*), ibn-Rushd recognizes the real function of the retina as receiving the image and transmitting it to the brain, and the fact that such diseases as smallpox leave immunity in those afflicted. His fame, however, rests on his commentaries on Aristotlean philosophy, which facilitated the understanding of the Greek philosopher to Arabic and Latin readers. Ibn-Rushd knew no more Greek than his Moslem predecessors; he used translations of Aristotle and of his commentators. He became the "commentator" as Aristotle was "the teacher." What he produced, however, were not commentaries in our sense of the term; they were treatises using in part the titles of Aristotle's works and paraphrasing their contents. Beginning in the 1230s, they were translated and revised repeatedly into Hebrew and Latin in Naples, Toledo, and other European cities. They more than any other works made Cordova the Athens of the West. The school of studying and understanding Aristotle through Averroës, known as Averroism, remained dominant in Europe from the thirteenth to the sixteenth centuries. Its influence became manifest in Talmudists and in Scholastics such as Thomas Aquinas. As for his coreligionists, ibn-Rushd was no more acceptable than his earlier confrere ibn-Sina (Avicenna). His views on the world's eternity, predestination, and the resurrection of the body sharply conflicted with those of the revelation.

A contemporary and fellow Cordovan of ibn-Rushd was ibn-Maymun (Maimonides), the most celebrated Jewish physician and philosopher in the entire Arab period and reputedly the most celebrated Jewish scholar in the middle ages. In 1165, when thirty years old, ibn-Maymun's family, under Muwahhid persecution, moved to Cairo, where he became physician to Saladin and there he died in 1204. Ibn-Maymun studied under Arab scholars and wrote almost all his books in Arabic. Like ibn-Rushd he knew no Greek. Following the Moslem precedent he tried to bring Rabbinical Judaism into harmony with philosophy as understood and modified by his Moslem colleagues. With ibn-Rushd and ibn-Maymun the series of creative Arabic authors in the West may be said to have come to an end.

VI

Arab geographers and chroniclers were no less extravagant in their descriptive rhetoric of the caliphal capital in Europe than of its five forerunners in Asia and Africa. The fact that it was utterly lost to Islam may have made them more nostalgic. Some of them added "may Allah return it to Islam" when mentioning its name. In his comprehensive history of Moslem Spain the Maghribi historian al-Maqqari (d. 1632) included, in praise of Cordova, numerous quotations in prose and verse illustrated by the following:

Said a learned man from al-Andalus:
"Cordova surpasses all cities of the world in four principal features: its bridge over the Guadalquivir, its mosque, its palace al-Zahra', and above all, the sciences cultivated therein."[3]

Said al-Razi [Andalusian historian, d. 935]:
"Cordova the mother of cities, the navel of al-Andalus, the seat of royalty in ancient and modern times, in pre-Islam and Islam; its river is the largest in al-Andalus; its bridge is the wonder of the world in its architecture and design; its mosque is second to none in al-Andalus even in Islam."[4]

A poet has well said:
"Mention not Baghdad with all its glittering magnificence,

3. Al-Maqqari, *Nafh al-Tib min Ghusn al-Andalus al-Ratib*, ed. Ihsan 'Abbas, vol. I (Beirut, 1968), p. 153.

4. *Ibid.*, p. 460.

> And do not magnify the lands of Persia and China;
> For nowhere is there like Cordova a place,
> Nor in the world a man like ibn-Hamdin."[5]

Wrote al-Hijari (Andalusian historian, d. 1188):

Cordova after the conquest of the Iberian Peninsula became the ultimate goal of the land, headquarters of the army, mother of all towns, seat of the virtuous and pious, and the abode of the people of intellect and learning. Under the Marwanids [Umayyads] it served as throne of the caliphate, heart of the entire region, cupola of Islam and home of the imam. To al-Andalus it was as the head is to the body and the chest to the loin. Unto it flocked seekers of science and poetry, for it was a resort of the noble and a mine of the learned. In it book writers vied with warriors, and nobility mingled with military. From its horizon rose stars for the world, notables for the age. In it were composed exquisite books and issued unsurpassed writings. The explanation of the superiority of Cordovans over all others past and present lies in the fact that the city's climate is one of research and investigation in the variety of sciences and literature.[6]

When a shaykh from Cordova visited the Cordovan blind poet abu-Bakr al-Makhzumi (d. after 1164), then a Toledo resident, the poet asked him to come near so he could smell the breeze of his native town by smelling and kissing his head. He then dictated the following verses of his extemporaneous composition:

> O Cordova the beauteous! am I ever going to see you again?
> Will that day ever draw nigh?
> May the clouds ever enrich with rain your western quarters,
> While thunderstorms break over your lofty trees.
> You, whose nights are dawns, whose fields are luxuriant growths,
> And whose soil smells amber and rose.[7]

---

5. *Ibid.*, p. 459. Ibn-Hamdin was an independent ruler of the city in the war between the Murabits and Muwahhids.

6. Extracted from three quoted versions in al-Maqqari, pp. 153, 460–461.

7. Al-Maqqari, p. 155; cf. translation in Pascual de Gayanagos, *The History of the Mohammedan Dynasties in Spain* (London, 1840), vol. I, pp. 31–32.

Singular Arab caliphal capital in Europe, mighty seat of a Moslem dynasty, bride of al-Andalus, luminous center of intellectual activity, home of the highest civilization ever attained by Islam, bearer aloft of the torch of enlightenment amidst encircling gloom, Qurtubah served as a bridge for transmitting elements of Eastern culture to the West.

Bibliography and Index

Bibliography

Burckhardt, John L. *Travels in Arabia*. London, 1829.
Coke, Richard. *Baghdad the City of Peace*. London, 1927.
Coulson, N. J. *A History of Islamic Law*. Edinburgh, 1964.
Cressey, George B. *Crossroads: Land and Life in Southwest Asia*. Chicago, 1960.
Dodge, Bayard. *Al-Azhar: A Millennium of Muslim Learning*. Washington, 1961.
Dozy, Reinhart. *Spanish Islam*, tr. Francis G. Stokes. London, 1913.
Fakhri, Majid. *A History of Islamic Philosophy*. New York, 1970.
Fedden, Henry R. *English Travellers in the Near East*. London, 1958.
Fisher, W. B. *The Middle East*. 4th ed. London, 1961.
Hogarth, D. G. *The Penetration of Arabia*. New York, 1904.
Hourani, Albert H., and S. M. Stern, eds. *The Islamic City: A Colloquium*. Oxford & Philadelphia, 1970.
Lane-Poole, Stanley. *A History of Egypt in the Middle Ages*. 4th ed. London, 1968.
_____. *The Moors in Spain*. London, 1897.
_____. *The Story of Cairo*. London, 1906.
Lapidus, Ira M. *Muslim Cities in the Later Middle Ages*. Cambridge, Mass., 1967.
Levy, Reuben. *A Baghdad Chronicle*. Cambridge, 1929.
_____. *The Social Structure of Islam*. Cambridge, 1957.
Le Strange, Guy. *The Lands of the Eastern Caliphate*. Cambridge, 1930.
_____. *Baghdad during the Abbasid Caliphate*. Oxford, 1924.
Lloyd, Seton. *Twin Rivers*. Oxford, 1961.
Margoliouth, David S. *Cairo, Jerusalem and Damascus: Three Chief Cities of the Egyptian Sultans*. New York, 1907.
Ralli, Augustus. *Christians at Mecca*. Chicago, 1960.
Rutter, Eldon. *Holy Cities of Arabia*. London, 1928.
Stark, Freya. *Baghdad Sketches*. New York, 1938.
Von Grunebaum, Gustave E., ed. *Unity and Variety in Muslim Society*. Chicago, 1953.
Walzer, Richard. *Greek into Arabic: Essays on Islamic Philosophy*. Oxford, 1962.
Watt, W. Montgomery. *Islam and the Integration of Society*. Evanston, Ill., 1961.
_____. *Muhammad, Prophet and Statesman*. London, 1961.
Whishaw, Bernard and Ellen. *Arabic Spain*. London, 1912.
Wiet, Gaston. *Cairo: City of Art and Commerce*, tr. Seymour Feiler. Oklahoma, 1964.
Ziadeh, Nicola. *Damascus under the Mamluks*. Oklahoma, 1964.

Index

DATE DUE